The Ancient Bones Of Ceremony

By Tasara Jen Stone

ISBN-13: 978-1-7331378-0-5

Library of Congress Control Number: 2019907330

Published by Littleight Press
Editing and gracious book midwifery by Karin de Weille
Text and Cover Design by Tasara Jen Stone
Graphic editing by Tasara Jen Stone

Ceremonial photography by Carol Canterbury, Tasara Jen Stone. Allison Gee
took the photo of Carol playing her didgeridoo. Ken Duhe took the one of
Steve lifting his little girl in the air.

Author photograph by anonymous Samaritan, fellow passionate tree-lover
in the park.
All other photography by Tasara Jen Stone.

Disclaimer: Some ceremony examples come from real experiences, some are
fictional, some are a blend of both. All of the personal ceremony examples
are fictional. Interactions in the stories about public ceremony planning
are, of course, a product of my memory and interpretation. Photographs
of ceremonies are from very public events where photographing was
acceptable. Even so, faces and bodies have been altered to hide the identity
of individuals.

*For all spiritual teachings are deep remembrances of who we are,
and the things we already know.*

THE ANCIENT BONES
OF CEREMONY

REMEMBERING THE HEARTFELT WAYS

This is Carol's, so you better give it back.

TASARA JEN STONE

TASARA

TABLE OF CONTENTS

INVOCATION

We come to this sacred place,
standing, present in our yearning
to bring forth our own beauty and to hear it answered.

We call on our love for the winds, the plains, the high rock,
the forest, the oceans and all the precious places
we hold dear on this beautiful planet.

We call on the spirits that look over us,
whether we sense them or not,
our guardian angels, our faerie godmothers.

We call on the Great Blue Whale,
whose presence resounds with the gift
of dreaming and ancient knowledge.

We burn in our hearts,
the need for soulful ceremony.

Come to us, Spirits of Kindness.
Please hold us for this time of teaching.
With ease, may our wisdom be remembered.

May we return to wholeness and joy in our lives.
May we find healing in our song unearthed.
May we give back.

THE CIRCLE IS OPEN

We have come to the place of the great tree,

where earth meets sky and the spider travels between.

It is a place where the hoot of an owl means many things, and

a blazing sunrise can empty a long-forgotten cave.

The waters here have many voices, and the rushes are gossips.

Our footsteps can be heard by all the creatures who live here.

We cannot move without being seen.

We are entering the mysteries of sacred ceremony. Open yourself to receive the harmonies of Mother Earth's orchestral song. Find rich relations with the spirits of kindness that walk always beside us. Move freely to the otherworlds, beyond and back, as you search for answers, for mending and the weaving of love in your earthly home.

We are leaving on a journey together. We have donned our warm cloaks, our packs are set, and the morning air kisses our skin. The path we will take heads down to a pool, where lie the ancient bones of ceremony that our ancestors left for us. We will take up the bones, and as we continue our walk, they will sing to us about what we need to survive.

On our journey, you will craft a ceremony to nourish your life's passage, be it releasing, be it initiation, be it blessing or clearing. Then, when you have learned all that you can learn, we will return, bringing the magic home where it is needed the most. We will share our findings with others and then together, we will build a better world.

Lend me your ear and as we walk, I will tell you a story.

THE SONG OF CEREMONY

Long ago, in ancient times, the humans sang with the earth, as her songs emanated from the rush of the wind, the babbling of brooks and the patter of wolves' feet. Every creature had its own song, and all the songs wove together into a great orchestra. Through all this, wound a sacred, spiral path that all beings, then and now, travel upon.

This spiral path holds all the wisdom of life and death. It leads upwards in an arc of excitement and growth. It slows as it reaches the top, and then it bends down in quiet reverie. It continues, until it falls into darkness, where we are led through death's warm sleep. Finally, with longing, the path rises again. It reaches from gestation to seedling, and then it leaps, to form a new spiral. The path never returns. Always, it extends further.

Back then, people knew that to live fully meant to sing in harmony with the changes of the curved road. To run ahead, or to drag behind, meant to fall out of the greater song–this song which was so delicately held by the ongoing, melodic conversations between humans, spirits, animals, birds, mountains, the winds, and the rocks and rivers.

When someone died, there was a song. When a newborn came, there was a song. In times of crisis, when rhythm was lost, new songs were made to reweave the whole. The humans would dance then, for it gave them more power. They would clap their hands and raise their voices, and in response, the forces of life and death would come into balance. This was their way. It was so integral to their lives, they had no word for it.

Ah, ceremony. Ceremony happened when seeds were planted, when baskets were woven, and when a creature was hunted. Alongside this, were songs of relationship, which streamed through the everyday.

Dear Raven, in the high tree, I greet you.

Morning sun, your warmth makes me smile.

The hearth fire crackles, she tells me a secret.

I hear you, soft hills, 'be there in a while!

The many ceremonies, enacted over time and with repetition, gained a life of their own. They ebbed and flowed, rose in the air, and swept from people to people across the planet, mixing, enriching, season upon season. The rites became steeped in wisdom, imbued with the souls of all who practiced them. They flowered and whirled and kicked up a wind when called by the people, again and again.

Eons passed, and a whisperer came who told of grandeur and high places, while at the same time disparaging the downward curves of the spiral path. His whispers spread, until the humans stopped making songs of balance. Instead, they made songs of wealth and conquest, songs of straight lines, never turning. These songs became so popular that the humans started to believe they could reach a place, far away, where there was no death or darkness.

The souls of the living rites refused to answer the call of the new songs. Other spirits came who would, and the people's dances changed. The ancestral souls searched from town to town, lonely for the old ways. Not finding them, they burrowed themselves into the core of the earth, planning never to return.

The whisperer grew bolder. Now he no longer whispered. Instead, he shouted and tap-danced and made a spectacle of his vision of high, faraway places. This lured many humans from their homes. They followed the straight path and, in doing so, fell out of sync with the greater song. By rejecting the sacred spiral, they also rejected themselves. They lost their wholeness. And when they became hungry, they could not find nourishment. So instead, they stole what they needed from those with whom they used to sing. It was a terrible plight.

The few who remained on the spiral path sang urgent songs, calling their loved ones back, but mostly, they were drowned out by the cacophony. Persistent, they still sang, and they still practiced the old ceremonies. These humans remembered that 'people' meant all peoples, not just human peoples. They held onto their connection to the ancestral living rites and, through their efforts, kept them from disappearing into the earth forever.

Yet still, the enchantment of the shouter's song progressed until there was so much loss, that from *every* heart rose a yearning for the old ways. Collectively, this created a new, silent song, a calling for a song. It had the sort of silence you hear when a storyteller breathes in, and we all breathe in with her, right before she unfolds her story.

And now, here we are, a yearning people. Our relationship with the other creatures of the earth has waned, no longer in our every breath. Passing through childhood, we weren't given new songs of adulthood, or challenged by our elders. We weren't adorned by our mother, or witnessed by our family. Our place in this world isn't as sure, or as supported as it used to be.

But take comfort. Through layers of rock and dirt, the ancient rites have heard our call.

Unable to feign sleep anymore, they retraced their path, year after year, coming closer and closer to the earth's surface, until there they lay, nested at the bottom of a deep lake. Then, even more years passed. Mountains shifted rivers, and the lake became a pond. Finally, what was left of these rites could be seen, the ancient bones of ceremony.

I will take you to them.

But first I must warn you, though there is nothing left but bones, they are no ordinary bones. Their magic and wisdom have been so distilled, their voices ring with purity, and they sing and chatter like those who have been alone far too long. The lyrics to their songs have been lost, but these ancient bones speak volumes to those who don't need ears to listen.

The Ancient Bones

See the pool that we have come to, the mud along its edges.

Below is where they lie, the ancient bones of ceremony.
You see them glow, for there, is embedded wisdom.

Draw them from the water now, and gather them here, on this cloth.
Leave none behind, for each is essential.

You see, there is the Calling Bone. There is the Fire Bone to fuel our
work, and the Compass Bone to orient and draw circles. Here is the
Bridging Bone. It helps us to communicate with the otherworlds... There
is a song about the bones. I will sing it to you.

The Mother Bone Poem

The White Bone of Sacred Space,
the Compass Bone to claim our place.

The Bone of Intention marks the way,
to reach our aim, we cannot stray.

The Bridging Bone of symbols made,
its power sings where steps are laid.

The Calling Bone will bring them here,
whose blessed kindness holds us dear.

The Bone of Passion stokes the fire,
living breath of deep desire.

The Bone of Home to kiss the ground,
embrace this life to which we're bound.

The Bone of Honor knows our name,
as we know others, just the same.

The Hollow Bone for you and me
to blend our songs in harmony.

The Mother Bone who feeds us all,
the Mother Bone who holds us.
The Mother Bone who twines the road
and with her song unfolds us.

Now, let's bundle them up and we will be on our way. There is much to talk about before we bring out again.

Follow me under the trees, where we can talk. It is not good to chit-chat in sacred places.

Under the Trees

The foundations of ceremony are easily learned, yet never fully grasped. One can practice them for decades, and still they will shift and deepen, disappear and reappear. To keep learning, we have to stay present. We have to let go of what has worked in the past and trust that our bodies will retain the enduring truths we find. When we need new inspiration, we venture out to explore new methods, and then we return to the foundations. This spiral return is the way of Mother Earth in all her expressions. She grows, she learns, she dances, and then she rests, to contemplate a new dream once again.

Ceremony is a beautiful way to stay engaged with the transitions of our lives. Instead of letting life overwhelm us, we get up and dance life. We say yes. Yes, that happened, and yes, I feel. Yes, I have been changed, and yes, I have aspirations, too.

Restoring the practice of ceremony opens us to another lost, ancient tradition, which is story. We bring our personal dramas into sacred space, and suddenly, we have reclaimed authorship of our lives. We find meaning in how our struggles fit in with the greater song. We see our story as the great epic we know life should be, gilded letters and all.

We are on our way to the spiral path, where the landscape changes with every glance and curiosity unearths great secrets. To get there, we must take a trail that leads through our hearts. It is in that passage that we will find the first ingredient for sacred ceremony, our heart's hunger.

Part 1

Journey into Ceremony

INTO OUR HEARTS

What aches in you?

What yearns to be called forth?

What needs to be said?

What needs to let go?

Hunger is a burning fire in our core, a longing, an aching, sometimes a great sorrow. Our need creates a vacuum that pulls things to us. When nothing comes, the burning continues and the vacuum only gets bigger. This is not weakness. It is a natural reaction to imbalance. Our heart's hunger is wisdom. When we listen closely, we are shown what needs to be uncovered and attended to.

One doesn't need to have a religion or defined spiritual practice in order to perform ceremony, for the spirits of kindness are not bound by any social construct. One doesn't need to know how to work with crystals, or know the difference between using sage and sweet grass in order to have ceremony. One doesn't even need to travel to faraway places or believe in a deity at all. All one needs is the desire to bring an aspect of life that calls for attention into sacred space and give it the love it needs.

So, ask yourself. What aches in you? What yearns to be called forth? What needs to be said? What needs to let go? What? What? The answer may come quickly. Or it may take time. It starts with how you feel.

My friend and I had an argument and ever since, things haven't felt right.

And moves to what you need and want.

We need a fresh start, or we fear our friendship will not survive. We want to create a safe space together so we can voice our feelings, ask each other clarifying questions, and ceremonially put our feelings to rest.

Every one of our activities, structures and relationships go through the cycle of growth, decline, death and dreaming in some way. On any turn of this spiral, there is an opportunity for ceremony, not just at the junctures our overculture acknowledges, like baptism, graduation and marriage, but also with divorce, job change and new stages in our personal development. Listen. Perhaps one of those turns is asking for a ceremony.

I have been grieving alone for so long, I feel as if I will stagnate and die.

When you have it, it might be just a whisper of a feeling, so please elaborate. What needs to happen for you? And very importantly, why? Listen deep. Deep. Feel the pull in your body and draw the words out.

16

I imagine a light shining on my grief, allowing me to move on. Yes, I want to be seen and heard by my community. I know it would make me feel better.

Even if there is an obvious ceremony at hand, such as a wedding or a funeral, there will still be questions to answer, to make it personally meaningful for those involved. For example, some couples think of a wedding as a blending of souls. Others want to keep their individuality while making a bond of commitment. Some people need to openly grieve a death; others need to loudly celebrate their loved one's life.

I am going to be a new mom and feel like my entire personality is about to shift. I am afraid and confused. I want to address this so I can feel some excitement!

As you draw out your need and articulate your feelings, the roots of your ceremony are revealed.

I want to formally say goodbye to my active social life and set a strong intention for deepening the family nest. I need the recognition, support and wisdom of my community, and the blessings of my ancestor spirits. I feel this would help me in honoring and being more present to this amazing experience.

Sometimes, there is so much work involved in a transition, like moving our home, we forget to be present. We get caught up in planning, packing, hauling, and then as we settle into our new life, we barely realize what just happened. With ceremony, we put the cacophony of life on pause and honor our story. We give ourselves proper closure and free up energy, in order to embrace and face what is to come.

If your heart longs for a sacred event to replenish your life, but all you can feel is a jumble of muddled, difficult emotions, perhaps your ceremony needs to be about finding clarity, or even the courage to look within. Sometimes, we are so overwhelmed, we need a ceremony for the sole purpose of slowing down enough to find out what we need a ceremony for.

The ancient bones of ceremony will teach us how to sing in harmony with change, but the call for harmony comes from our hearts. We start the conversation, and the bones support us.

Your Heart

We have returned to the mystical pool where the bones of ceremony lay. Move closer to its edge and gaze upon the water. There, your thoughts are in the reflected patterns, skittering on the surface.

What does your heart call for?

I will be silent, and let you be still.

As you listen to your heart, ripples emerge from beneath. The surface patterns will break open and reveal the clarity you seek.

What does your precious heart call for? We take no more steps upon this journey until you are sure. Find what is vital and real for you. Choose with your heart, not with your mind. Write it all down, and fold it into your palm.

This is the way of ceremony. We whisper our yearning to the ancient bones, and then, in time, we receive an answer, in the form of a ceremony.

Now, take up the bundle and as we walk the spiral path, we will rattle the bones together. We will listen to their songs, allowing them to resonate in our bodies and fill us with new understanding.

The Song of the Bone of Intention

The Bone of Intention marks the way,

to reach our aim, we cannot stray.

The most powerful tool for ceremony is our will. After we sit with our hunger, we decide what action we will take to respond. This is our ceremonial intention.

The problem is, many of us don't think carefully enough about what we want, so when the time comes to throw ourselves behind our intentions, we have many ideas instead of one. Our energy becomes dispersed. Or, if we have unconscious feelings that contradict what we thought we wanted, our results are mixed or off the mark. Hence the warning, "Be careful what you wish for."

Actually, finding our intention isn't that difficult. It has already been shown to us by the longing in our hearts. We just need to look more closely. Take your heart's hunger through the following descriptions of ceremonial expressions and see what resonates with you.

Dropping into Ourselves and the Spiritual Realms

Sometimes our heart calls for inspiration, new direction. In this case, our ceremony-building efforts will be geared towards creating an environment free from distraction and conducive to deep trance.

In a group setting, this may look like a guided meditation. A leader takes us through a series of visualizations designed to bring us into a very relaxed state. Then the meditation can go in several directions. We might focus on clearing our own energy field, or we might be taken on a metaphorical journey, sometimes based on ancient mythology, using the power of archetypes. Some guided meditations lead us the entire way out and back. Others lead us to a point and then drop us off with a mission to complete the journey on our own. In communities where people have been trained in spirit journey, nothing is led at all. Drumming or rattling becomes the guide, and everyone knows how to get to where they need to go in order to find answers to their questions. After the journey, there may be a time for sharing experiences, either with the entire group or in pairs or small groups.

If we are needing a healing experience, it might be crafted into the guided meditation, or we may want to simply lie down and ask for healing from the spirits of kindness, with the help of a repetitive rhythm (drum, rattle, click sticks) to support our trance state.

Calling in Change

Sometimes we so badly need a new situation in our lives: a healthier relationship, a better home, a college acceptance. There is a lot we can do to obtain that on the physical plane, but we can also send out a signal for help in sacred ceremony. We use the energy of our need, that strong pulling feeling, to create an expression of our desire. It could be a sketch showing the kinds of loving interactions we wish to be having with others. It could be a written statement of the type of home we are looking for. It could be a song, exclaiming how important it is that we get accepted into college. Doing this in sacred space amplifies our need, sending a message into the world. It draws things to us. It also supports our everyday efforts towards change. When we do this work, we look only to affect ourselves, never others without their permission.

Passing Through the Portal

A portal-crossing–or initiation–is usually a gift, since much of the energy in the ceremony flows from the hearts of the community directly to the initiate. Great power comes from acknowledgment and witnessing. There are usually blessings as well, bestowed through thoughtful words, songs and symbolic gifts.

The moment of transformation for the initiate can happen by declaration, or with a walk across a symbolic boundary. It can happen with the gifting of new garments of station or a sacred talisman. When an initiate is asked to make their own statement, their intention and determination have great power. What is said in sacred space becomes a binding oath.

Sending Out

Sometimes our hearts are so full, they beg for release. We long to pour out our emotions. We have to let go of someone, something, or even a time in our lives. We have bursting love to send to our ailing friends, with their permission. We want to give praise to the spirits of kindness. We want to send a flow of peace and balance into the collective psychic common space.

We have written our prayers on colored paper.
Now, we place them in the flames.
Facing the center, we raise our arms together towards the sky.

Awoooooo!

We send our prayers to the spirits.
Our intentions take flight on the wind.

Let's consider our friend who is pregnant with her first baby. Her meditation has shown her that she wants to express her heart in three ways: a formal goodbye to her old life, a symbolic mark of moving forward, and a call to her ancestors for blessings.

For the formal goodbye part, will she read proclamations and then burn them, or will she speak directly to her friends? What will the proclamations be? How will the energy in her heart move?

For the symbolic moving-on, will she walk through a physical portal? Will she read a statement of commitment she has prepared, or will she dance her new life, discovering how it may be embodied? Will she trust that an expression will come in the moment?

For the final section of her ceremony, how will the ancestor spirits be called? What will she do when she opens herself to their blessing? Will she be lying down? Or will she channel them by drawing a picture that can be kept for further inspiration?

These questions are addressed early in the process because once the answers are clear, they will inform later choices about the colors to use or banners to fly or music to play. Always the focus is: "What will we do to address our heart's burning? What is the action we will take?"

Our new mother decides that indeed she will make proclamations of her intention to let go of the aspects of life she will not have time for anymore. She will also look for things to burn that represent those parts of her life.

Her friends have gotten involved in the ceremony planning now, and she has handed off the "new life" component to them. Though she doesn't know how it will happen, she knows that she will be crossing a threshold of some sort.

She has been seeing a vision in her mind for days of her heart cracking open and broadening to encompass the world. So, for the blessing part she will lie down and focus on that. Her friends will energetically support this in some way.

Let us now turn to our friend who wants a ceremony to help him move through his grief.

He says to himself, "Grief is not something I can just decide to be done with. It is a long, mysterious process that goes through many cycles. At the same time, I feel stuck and need help to allow my healing process to continue."

He thinks some more and realizes that he hasn't cried in months. In ceremony, he wants to express his grief fully and let go of the parts that he doesn't need anymore. This will make room for new feelings to arise. He also has a strong desire for gentle inspiration or grace to enter his life. He feels he will need help staying engaged in the world in the months after the ceremony. He is afraid of sinking into an insurmountable depression.

He wants to address his heart's needs in two ways: expressing/releasing the old grief and establishing a reconnection with the world that will sustain him through the rest of his grieving journey.

How will he express his grief? Will he read a poem he wrote? Will he say his goodbyes out loud? Will he release things by burning them in a fire? Will he stomp? Will he walk a walk of letting go?

He decides to keen. Even though he has not been able to cry, he knows that with witnesses it will be easier.

How will his connection to the world be restored? What personal ways work best for him?

Because drawing is something that has always been transformative for him, he decides to draw symbols that come to him in the moment, one to represent how he has been feeling and three to describe what a new life could be like for him.

Your Hunger

Dear friend, I will set my walking stick down and wait, while you revisit your heart.

Surround it with love. Answer its call with a plan. Do you need to send your energy out? Drop in for inspiration?

Put the book aside and honor yourself with this time. With your intention, you are setting the direction of the creative forces that make your ceremony sacred.

Wait until you know what is true for you.

Then, once you know what to do, blow your intention into a seed and place the seed in your pocket.

We cannot trek without this seed or there will be nothing to nourish. The pages will lose their magic, and the journey will not be true. The knowledge we are traveling through, it must be embodied!

When you are ready, with seed safely stored, we will pick up our sticks and walk together again, listening to the ancient bones of ceremony.

The Bridging Bone of Symbols Made

There is a bridge that spans the spirit realm and the one we live in. We walked across it when we were conceived. It's the same bridge our inspirations cross when we are creating. This bridge, it shimmers and winks, sliding between dimensions, appearing when we need it the most.

When we are doing ceremony, we make our own bridge with living symbols in order to manifest our intentions. Living symbols are potent actions, patterns, sounds and smells that carry the elements we want to have in our ceremony. They carry a presence that we interact with, and they serve as a conduit to bring our ceremony from the world of form to the unformed, and back again.

What do our eyes need to rest upon during our ceremony? Are there colors, textures, scents that evoke the emotions we are feeling or the spirits we will be calling? Does our work call for ultimate silence, or the steady beat of a drum? Should the room be cozy and nurturing, stark and simple, or outside in the brisk wind? Music and spoken word, created and expressed by you, are some of the most powerful ways to create a bridge to the spiritual realms.

Symbols allow our minds to rest and focus; they free us from the need to keep track of everything as we go. The effort we put into choosing and finding them is energy that makes our ceremony strong. Sometimes we want to have a feast of the senses; other times, we feel that less is more. Even if we don't use many physical items, our intention will need to be expressed in some sort of symbolic action.

This is the part that over time, enacted again and again in a community, becomes culture. These days, many people think of culture as logos, TV shows and business-funded parades, but that is not culture. That is corporate-sponsored garbage because those symbols often do not represent our values. Culture grows out of our interactions with each other and reflects our collective struggles and dreams. It is the expression of the hearts and minds of people through word, song, art, mannerism and lifestyle. It also has a beautiful way of mirroring the shapes and sounds of the land we live upon.

Organically grown culture is a precious thing that we have lost so completely in modern societies, we don't have a common, symbolic language that is not mired in commercialism or mass media messaging. Out of desperation, we look to ceremonies from indigenous cultures for meaning, but though their ideas may spark our creativity, using their specific ways is rightfully upsetting to the peoples of those cultures. Also, their ways don't have the impact for us that we know, in our bones, ceremony should have. This is because in traditional cultures, people have a relationship with their symbols and traditions that began at birth. If they don't, it is because their cultures have been stripped away by colonialism, oppression and systematic genocide. In this case, the meanings are equally personal and dear, for they now contain the rich history of reclaiming one's traditions. Cedar, for the tribes in the Pacific

Northwest of what is now called the United States, means everything to societies there. It was used by their ancestors for clothing, soup pots, baskets, canoes, homes, medicine and more. Buffalo is everything to the native people who live in the Midwest for similar reasons. Wouldn't it have been silly if the people who lived by the ocean did an annual Buffalo Ceremony? I can still honor the cedar trees, based on the way they calm me and clear my mind as I gaze up from under their boughs. I can dance to the beauty of their bright green skirts in the spring, but to bring in meanings from another culture wouldn't be honest.

Even though indigenous tribes have radically different cultural practices, what they do have in common is their personal, living, spiritual relationship to the land, the animals and trees. This relationship is not static; it is one of partnership on the sacred spiral road. All beings are considered neighbors and family.

We don't have to be native to an indigenous culture in order to find ceremonies that alter the course of our lives. We need to find symbolism for our own messy, modern lives. When we choose right, our heart feels a resonance and the room feels a little bigger. The resonance grows into song, vibrating along the bridge we built, and the bridge shimmers. Our breathing relaxes, and we know we are getting a little closer to home, for all spiritual journeys are deep remembrances of who we are and the things we already know.

*A group of people symbolizing the ocean healing
by dancing with sheer blue fabric*

By doing our ceremony this way, planning from the ground up, paying attention to our deepest longings and honing our intentions, we will never have any reason to borrow a rite from another culture.

Let us return to our friend, the new mother. Now that she has verbalized her intentions, the living symbolism of her ceremony falls into place.

She wants to emphasize the proclamation she makes, so she chooses a bell that her grandmother gave her. This actually works out great because she had wanted to use the bell, and now she knows how. Her grandmother passed away recently, and she has felt watched over by her love ever since. A fire is needed to burn papers of things she is letting go. She will burn old concert tickets, not because she will never go to a concert again, but to release the energy, keep her memories and start anew.

Her friends will create an archway out of their bodies for her to walk under. She will start off wearing high heels and will take them off after moving through the portal to ground herself into motherhood. At this point, her friends will wrap her in a shawl of red.

She chooses to do the ceremony beside a river because its qualities speak to her of motherhood. Dressed in her shawl, she will allow herself a long moment to feel the river and mystery of universal motherhood and surrender herself to it. She will let her feelings move her into a dance that will end in a river plunge, as a symbol of entering motherhood. Returning, she will lie down on a receiving blanket, which has an embroidered Goddess on it. It is a gift from her mother. Her friends will drum or rattle or play other kinds of music while she closes her eyes and waits for revelation and blessing.

When she is done receiving, she will sit up. Her friends will present her with gifts to support her motherhood and explain their meaning, one by one.

Much care has been put into discovering the intention and then custom-making this ceremony just for her. If our new mother had followed a ceremony she found in a book, it surely would have been helpful, even if just because of the energy spent enacting the ceremony, but it probably would not have been as powerful because it wouldn't have touched on her unique, intimate needs.

Our grieving friend keeps seeing a vision in his mind of grieving as being an ocean. When asked *why* it is like an ocean, he replies,

> *"Grief is overwhelming and beautiful at once. It is too big to find any direction, though I know there are currents somewhere. It seems like something to surrender to in order to survive."*

So, he chooses to do his ceremony at the ocean. Because of this, he can draw his symbols in the sand. He already knows that one will be an enclosed shape expressing his isolation. Another will be a flow of curves, showing the current of healing and change he is trying to reach.

When he is finished, he will sit up and meditate on the rolling waves, allowing their sound, shapes and motion to speak to him. He will focus on his desire to keep his creativity alive as he continues through his chapter of grief and will search for divine messages in the landscape.

Your Visions

We rest once more on our journey.

That seed in your pocket is trembling with new life...

It is time to gather your tools and plan the enactment of your intentions. Make your decisions and then pack them into a bundle and store them away. I will build a fire for you, humming a tune of traveling, and put on a pot for stew.

We have come far together if you have been dreaming as we walked. If you have not, I suggest you go back to visit our last stopping points and call to your dreams. Pick up the trail and begin once more. I will be here.

We are about to climb a high pass.

The White Bone
of Sacred Space

I have chosen this place because I love it, and it is so beautiful. I am sure you will find a spot that speaks to you. Ceremonial grounds need to be special, not to the world, but to you. We choose our place and the land sings. We create a sanctuary at home and the room embraces us.

Once our ceremony is planned, it starts to vibrate with a life of its own. Energy builds as we get closer to ceremonial grounds. Is it our anticipation? Is our ceremony speaking to us so soon? Do you hear that voice coming from the canyon below? I believe all of this is true.

Now that we are finally here, in the place of your choosing, let us create a sacred space for ceremony. Sacred means set apart, entitled to reverence and respect. On this occasion, we are setting a special place just for us, for tending to our heart's needs. Physically, sacred space is the area that we mark off before we begin ceremony. Spiritually, it is the invisible boundary that establishes who is welcome from both the physical and spirit realms. It contains our intentions, our magical tools and, once we invite them, the spirits of kindness.

The contained nature of sacred space protects the purity of our intentions and serves as an amplifier. Our attention is keener. What is said has more impact. What occurs has a lasting effect on our future. We create the space, we fill it, and then, with all the mixing of the elements, alchemy happens. When we are finished, we dissolve its boundaries and return the place back to the land.

Preparing the Physical Space

Let's clean up a bit. See if you notice any stones or branches that can be set aside. We want it to feel clear in here. If we were home, we'd remove items not relevant to our intentions so as not to be distracted.

Lay your tools of ceremony in the circle. Create your altar if you are going to use one. We might want to mark the boundaries of our space with stones or other items. As we do this, a subtle shift occurs on the spiritual plane.

Preparing Ourselves for Ceremony

Now, on the precipice of diving into the magic, we will tend to the primary instrument of our alchemical work, ourselves. It is our minds, bodies, breath and emotions that guide our intention towards the culmination of our ceremony, so we have to be clear inside ourselves. We want to make sure that unconscious emotions and thoughts don't take us off track.

If there were many of us here, we'd stop socializing, shake our bodies out and get present. Someone might talk us through a brief meditation to help us shed the everyday hassles of life, or at least put them resolutely outside the door. This is something I want you to know how to do. There are many ways to do it, and a plethora of resources out there for you to explore, so I will mention just one fundamental concept, which is grounding.

Grounding

Grounding is about 'coming to earth.' In modern society, we spend much of our time living in our minds, so we need to call ourselves fully into our bodies before we venture forth. Then we extend our senses out to what is around us. The richness of the physical realm, when we are aware, holds infinite portals into the sacred realms.

When we enter sacred realms, our awareness will become even more heightened. This is highly desired in ceremonial practice, but we still need to keep our bearings. Otherwise, our visions and profound experiences may slip away like dreams.

Being grounded means being rooted in the richness of our central reality while at the same time having circuits running to the spiritual realms below and above. This is why so many traditions use the visualization of merging with a tree when they ground. It means being attuned to multiple sources of knowing while not being rocked from our center. Just as a ground-wire sends an overload of electric charge to the earth, being grounded can prevent us from becoming spiritually overwhelmed or short-circuited. The more grounded we are, the more potent the energy and the broader the array of information we are able to hold in our consciousness, and, as a result, the greater the healing we are able to retrieve from the spiritual realm. Over time, as our physical tolerance for spiritual energies increases, we are able to sustain clarity for longer, more powerful experiences.

There are many grounding exercises offered by a variety of traditions and authors. I will give you a powerful, barebones method. I will say it in short form instead of trying to talk you through the meditation. This way, you can put the book down and do it yourself, at your own pace.

Grounding Meditation

Do something, anything, to bring your awareness to your body. Stretching, shaking and silliness are highly encouraged. Move your body in whatever way it wants to move. If you are able, get up on your feet. If not, move whatever part of your body you can—your arms, your head, your shoulders, your chest.

Do it. Feel it.

Spiritual work is body work. If we let our minds do everything, we really miss the boat. Let's get out of our heads.

After this, stand or sit tall and simply call all parts of yourself back to your body.

Reel them in like a fishing line.

Slap your sides and face and say your name out loud.

Dance around a bit more and make goofy faces.

Then when you have about had it with that, get calm and close your eyes.

Settle in. Imagine a ball of light in your chest. Really get into it.

Spend a minute knowing it there in your chest, and then let the ball slowly drift down through your core and into the earth.

Go far, very far, through the mantle and into the sacredness below, the earth's energetic, nourishing well.

Drink from this well, this over-flowing well. There is enough for everyone, so take as much as you need, and when you are done, rest there and notice how it feels.

Allow your ball of light to slowly rise through all those levels until it comes up right below you, into your body and rises through your core to rest in your heart.

Be with this for a moment, and notice how it feels to be in your center while at the same time, having awareness of the nourishment of the deep.

Now, allow your ball of light to slowly rise, through your upper core, out of the top of your head and above.

Follow the ball of light as it rises higher, through the stratosphere, past the cosmos and into the sacredness above, which is filled with blessings. These, too, are never depleted.

Allow these blessings to stream into you through the channel your ball of light has created. Remain here as long as you need to, and when you have been filled with what you need, notice how you feel.

Allow the ball of light to slowly travel back down through the layers, through your head and down, into your heart.

Notice how it feels to be in your center, in your heart and at the same time feeling the great pathway that goes from the divine nurturing above, through your core, to the divine nurturing below.

You are in neither of these places but in yourself.

You are a midpoint between earth and sky.

Now allow the two energies from below and above to merge with each other, right in your heart.

KaBAM!

A shockwave happens, and it rushes from you horizontally, in all directions!

You are here. You are the midpoint to all places.

You are at the crossroads, the place where things happen. You are in your place on the earth's surface, and you are ready.

Open your eyes.

Notice how it feels. Notice how the world looks.

This is what it is like to be grounded.

Now you are awake. You are ready to begin your work.

The Compass Bone
to Claim our Place

As grounded people, we are now in conscious relationship to the place where we will be creating sacred space.

Pick up the Compass Bone. It holds two gifts, the compass that gives us direction, and the drafting compass that we will use to draw a circle of safety around us. We want to create an environment that supports vulnerability because when we are truly open, we can be truly changed. We want to facilitate a heartfelt conversation between our deepest selves and the spirits of kindness. This risk, this challenge is before us, to take our weathered warrior shields and leave them at the door, so we do it.

We are about to draw our circle. Look around. Feel the quiet power of your groundedness running through you. Look to the North. What is there? Smell it. Feel it. If you were inside a building or structure, what would you know is on the other side of the wall, even miles from you, to the North? Is it city? Forest? The arc of a river? Don't make pictures of what you think North should mean in a metaphorical way. When we lay the groundwork for a ceremony, we orient ourselves to the live world. Do this for the East, the South, the West.

I am here, that is there.

I am the center of the compass.

I am putting my stakes down.

I am claiming my space for ceremony.

I am not separate from the planet.

I am of it and this is my action.

Many cultures associate specific spirits or additional qualities with the directions, and these would be honored at this time. Doing so invokes the influence and power of greater mysteries and archetypal influences. We ask them to witness and support our coming journey into the spiritual realms. For example, if you come from a tradition where the East is associated with innocence, when something unexpected happens in the East quarter of the circle during the ceremony, it may be interpreted through the lens of innocence.

Not all cultures agree on the directional associations, nor should they because they come from completely different regions of our wild planet. One region may have an ocean to the North while the ocean is West from your home. Another region may have summer during your winter. One sure thing is that the sun rises in the East and sets in the West; it would be easy to associate East with the beginning of things and the West with endings. If you live in the Northern hemisphere, then North would be cold, or night, or death, whereas South is midday, heat and the peak of things.

Sometimes associations are highly personal. For instance, maybe when you were young, you drove east on a long road trip and you hit a deer. You got out of the car and went up to the deer, and while it passed away, it looked through you and you felt your body chill. Ever since, the direction of East will always mean invoking the spirit of the deer. Or maybe you spent years watching your children play from your northern, kitchen window and because of that, your circle always has the spirit of play come from the North.

Many people also associate the directions with the elementals of Fire, Earth, Water, Air and more. We will enter those mysteries together on a further leg of our journey.

That said, this step of defining directional associations is not necessary for a powerful ceremony. Work with what makes sense to you instead of reaching outside yourself for meaning. What is most important as you begin your ceremony is that you orient yourself to the physical world and create a non-physical boundary.

Now take your compass and draw that circle.

A circle is a natural thing to draw to claim one's space. It's been done all over the world for millennia. Some people do it by walking around their space or by drawing a literal line in the sand. Some place stones or other items along the boundary. Some hold a stick in their hand, stand in the center and draw in the air as they turn their bodies. Some people do not physically mark the space but proclaim it with their words while marking with their eyes the edges of the area they are claiming.

Schwoo!

This is a safe space.

May no person or presence enter this space uninvited.

Only the benevolent are welcome here.

We have done it. Sacred space is set, and now the boundary around us has become an energetic container. What is said and done here will imprint itself on our psyches, altering the shapes of our thoughts, creating repercussions in our lives and rippling out to the rest of the world.

We want to behave in ways that are responsible to the power that will be built here. We also want to make sure that energies and spirits inside the container are relevant and supportive to our best interests. Just as we were picking up stones and branches to clear the space, now we will do an energetic clearing.

Metaphysical Clearing

The deeper we go into creating sacred space, the more our consciousness will shift. This heightened state makes it a lot easier to tell if anything feels off. It isn't a special ability. It's the same thing we sense in a room after a stuffy, boring meeting, or after two people have had an argument. Energy needs to be aired out sometimes, the psychic clutter swept.

There isn't a right way to do this. A space can be energetically cleared with sound: the clapping of hands, bells, singing, and proclamations of intent. It can be cleared with motion, like a dance or 'air sweeping' with a broom. I gift you with the playful song I like to use with my broom.

Out with the old! In with the new!

Out with the old! In with the new!

I also like to spin in circles with my arms spread, to whoosh the energies out. Spaces can be cleared by burning herbs that have been known to work like this for ages—sage, cedar, mugwort. Sometimes, the space tells me what it needs. A very effective way to clear the space is to ask our spirits of kindness to do it, and then drum for them as we witness. We can even ask the spirits to prepare sacred space many days before the ceremony. They love to do this and have ways that we cannot imagine.

How you want to treat moving in and out of sacred space is up to you. Some groups do not allow participants to leave or enter once the circle is set. Some have a designated person who will cut a doorway in the air for you, say, if you need to leave to go to the bathroom. Others will ask you to open it for yourself in a formal or informal way. Others do not pay attention at all. You will learn your way.

Once we have drawn our circle, we have begun our journey. We have reached the edges of the mundane. We have stepped closer into mystery, strengthening our focus and intent. We have literally created a boundary that unwanted energies cannot cross. This will hold us in our work, like the sheltering cloak of the universal mother.

The Calling Bone
to Bring Them Here

Invocations – Filling the Container

We may have already invited some helpful energies in, when we marked the directions and drew our circle. Now we will make formal invitations to the spirits of kindness, in whatever way spirit is understood to be true for you. We are hailing their friendship and also asking for their assistance. Some people like to do this when they arrive at ceremonial grounds. Some like to wait until their space is clear. Others do invocations at both times, including setting out symbols of the elements and spirits.

For those of you who are not working with spirits but will be using the power of the elements to fuel your ceremony, now is a great time to invoke them while verbalizing your intentions. If it feels too rote or stilted to say it out loud, and you don't have people following you who need to know what's going on, open your heart and make strong, silent invocations.

I call upon the morning sun, ever in your beauty.
Please witness my ceremony
and fuel it with your rising.

I honor the memory of my grandmother.
Wherever you are, please hear my words
as I send you my love today.

I invoke that day when everything went wrong.
Be present so that I may learn from your energies
and glean wisdom from my life.

We need to be specific about who we are inviting for blessings and assistance because the spirit worlds are just as complex and various as the physical world. They are full of all sorts of characters. Some have our best interests in mind; some have agendas of their own; some are just primal forces that do one thing. If we make a generic call out into space without specifying who we are talking to, there is no way of knowing who will answer back. It's like being in a chat room online. We don't know how old the other person is, what they've lived through, whether they are just trying to rile us up, or if they are trying to get us to download something that will infect our computer. It's the same in the spirit world, so we keep common sense in both realms.

So, call out to your guardian angel or faerie godmother, or other helping spirits you know and love. Thank them. Open your mind to let them know what your intentions are. Ask them to help you stay on track and

to contribute their energy to your efforts. If you don't know your helping spirits by name, you can call generically but specify that you are only
inviting those that have your best interests in mind.

*I now open my space to the compassionate spirits who love me and
desire to bring healing to me and my loved ones.*

*Archetypal grandmother, who has been by my side,
please bless this space with your presence,
support me in my work and keep my intentions clear.*

*Guardian spirits, wherever you may be,
I have felt your presence for years and
I am grateful for your protection.
I invite you to join me.*

*I am celebrating the coming of Spring!
I invite all the benevolent faeries,
who nourish all beings under their care, to join us.
Let us play. Let us dream.
Let us feed the land together with our song.*

Notice that there isn't any commanding going on here. Our relationships with the spirits are reciprocal, not hierarchical. They do not come
at our bidding, and we do not grovel before them. It is true that our
experiences with the compassionate spirits can be so profound, they
inspire devotion, but that is very different from making oneself lower
or smaller. The spirits truly love us and want us to feel our own divine
spark. The compassionate spirits always want to come to our loving
ceremonies! Their only agenda is to bring healing into the world, and
they can't do it without us as conduits and witnesses.

Some traditions like to put food and flower offerings outside the circle
for the spirits that are not welcome. Not only does that send some love,
but it also appeases them.

This is a great time for incense and the lighting of candles. The type
you choose will depend upon your intention.

What sacred ingredients will resonate with your intention and bring your ceremony to life? Rose petals? The light of the rising sun? Candles of white? The rush of the waterfall? The passion of Kali? Who, what do you need to call?

The Bone of Passion
Stokes the Fire

Through the practice of claiming space, marking a circle and inviting the spirits of kindness, our ceremonial ground has been transformed. The air feels charged. We are betwixt and between the mundane and the spirit worlds, in that sweet spot, that place where our hearts are heard by the many unseen, where we can touch upon the delicate threads of the great web that spans us all. Our consciousness has shifted into trance, our senses are opened to deeper realms of the subconscious and to the realms of spirit. We are ready.

It is time to add the fuel we need to fulfill the intention of our ceremony. We are inviting the last guest—our passion. We have been carefully carrying our feelings through this whole process, and now we express them. This is the moment when we might feel a rush to pour out the energy that has been building inside us. It might also be a time when we need to push ourselves through a small barrier of inhibition to get moving. In this culture, where we are taught to adore those on stage and disparage our own creativity, too many of us have become frozen, our emotions and thoughts so compacted under our skin, it is difficult to express ourselves and feel safe.

Gently or fiercely, whatever you are feeling about your ceremony, express it. Say it. Dance it. In sacred space, we don't worry about what we look like. We want our energy to flow so it can be transformed, so we move our bodies. Healing happens in flow.

Stomp it if you are mad. Walk it. Sway in your chair if you can't stand. Move your arms. Let the beat of the drum open your awareness and lead you on. Pick up a rattle and make noise. Speak your truth about why you are here. You might be surprised at how much energy is trapped under your skin once you begin to let it out.

Awoo! Awoo!

I am here! I am here!

I ride in my passion, intentions are clear.

Energy can come out in a fierce declaration of personal sovereignty. It can pour from us in tears of gratitude, a gentle cry, a howl of grief. It can be raised through the slow build of a community song. A surprising amount can be released with a subtle, potent gesture. Sometimes, the symbolic actions and intentions we planned are already so high-energy, we don't need to add anything more.

Our sacred container fills with raw, heartfelt energy, waiting to be released when we aim the arrows of our intentions and let them fly.

Sending Our Intentions

Just as a musician senses the peak of an improvisation, we feel it when the energy is most potent, and it is time for enactment. There is that moment when the building slows and we know that if we don't act, the tide will subside. If we choose, we can allow the energy to rise and fall a few times before acting, as long as we intend to sustain our activities through each cycle and not rest too much between them. Each cycle will pull us deeper into trance. Raw emotion becomes clarified into pure energy, protecting our intention from any anger or despair we may have expressed. The signal to move into action is when we become crystal clear in our minds, with power running through our bodies, and we know there is nothing else to do.

When we reach this place, if we begin to feel difficulty maintaining focus, we throw ourselves into our plan. The Bone of Intention has been leading us all the way up to this point, and it will guide us through to the end. We step forward. We speak our words. We break our bonds. We cross the threshold. We offer ourselves to spirit for insight. A valve is opened and the energy we have raised rushes forth, honed by our intention.

We hold this opening until there is no more to flow, and then we step back. Our body listens and at this time, a response comes, whether slight or astounding, from deep inside us or from the natural world around us or from the realm of spirit. It could be an answer. It could be a new feeling of peace. It could be a confidence in the clarity that our full intentions have been successfully sent. We are in a place where, in complete trust, we don't look back.

The work is done. Everything now is in the hands of spirit.

A gust blows through and lifts the leaves.

The air has never been so sweet.

Blessed is the time we've spent,

Blessed the ground beneath our feet.

C

The Bone of Home
to Kiss the Ground

The pivotal moment in a ceremony takes only a few minutes, but it wouldn't happen at all without our mindful planning, grounding and marking of sacred space. Just as we carefully created layer upon layer to enter our dance, we now must release the energies, layer by layer.

We call ourselves home. We steer our container back to the mundane, the place where we understand the rules, keep our clothes and cook our food. We return all excess energy back to the earth's core to be used for creating life in other ways. This is called grounding the ceremony.

It would not be a proper end to a party without goodbyes and thank yous, so we end this one by thanking the spirits and elements and ancestors of the land.

We give gratitude to the Spirits of Kindness for helping us.
We give gratitude to the elements and directions.

We take a moment to quench our soul-thirst by drawing as much of
the left-over energy as we need into our bones.
There is enough for everyone.
When we are ready, together we place our hands on the ground and

send the rest safely home.
Home to the earth, to the ones we pray for, to Mother Ocean.

We raise our hands up and send the rest safely home,
to breeze, to cloud, to sky.

We come home ourselves, back to our bodies,
for some of us have been traveling in the other-realms.
We close the portals to the spirit worlds
and we embrace the mundane.

Say your name out loud, pat your body, your face, your head. The reason it is so important to return to the luscious, physical realm is that any gifts we may have received in our ceremony, be it through inspiration or vibration, need to be integrated into our everyday lives, if we want true change.

We also want to break our trance, so we are protected in the outside world. Being in trance is a lot like being intoxicated. We are more easily 'taken,' more likely to lean on old patterns from the past, less able to maintain healthy boundaries.

Someone makes a closing statement.

Someone draws back the invisible curtain that has been holding
our container, with a gesture.

The circle is open.

There is a crescendo of music. Or laughter.

We are grateful.

Blessed Be. Blessed Be. Blessed Be.

We have been fully present to a spiritual transformation, and now we bring that presence to the everyday. Later, when we rejoin our loved ones, our changed vibration will be transmitted to them without our having to say a word.

It is possible to come back but still feel buzzed and slightly altered because there is more spiritual information in our field than our psychology can digest at once. So, be gentle with yourself. Take care. Embrace the process. Food is good for grounding, too.

One terrific way to "bring the medicine home" is to journal. Trance state is much like dream state; it is easy for important details to slip away. As you start to collect memories and potent associations from previous ceremonies, journaling will create a rich history for you to look back at and learn from. Specific markers in your life become chapter headers; visionary characters that keep showing up become archetypes, and recurring themes will shape the story's through-lines. Imagine thinking of life in terms of 'before the rite of passage' and 'after the rite of passage,' instead of before the hardship and after the hardship. Rather than allowing suffering to define our lives, we've fully engaged with life's changes and found sustained meaning through our ceremonies.

Another wonderful way is to direct the energy and revelations into an art form. This provides multi-dimensional processing, as the new energy continues to develop through our work, going further than the ceremony could have taken it. Sometimes, the art becomes a gift to share with the rest of the world so that others may benefit from the medicine, too.

Ceremony can help us along in gentle ways, but ceremony can also move tectonic plates. If emotions come that are difficult to manage, we can seek assistance. Perhaps we need to talk to a friend. Maybe an energy worker can clear our field of old clutter. Maybe we need to book an appointment with a therapist or spiritual healer. The gift of having difficult emotions surface through ceremony is that we are finally able to embrace them and bring them home.

Your Initiation

Ah, we have stopped for the night, down the hill from the ceremonial grounds, under some broad maple trees. Our evening fire is built, supper is done, and finally, it is time for you to enact your ceremony. Once again, I will wait for you. I will wait all night long if I have to. I will keep the fires burning for you, and I will be praying for you.

This is the initiation I have planned for you. There is no going back after this, and there is no going forward until you have done it.

So, set out on your own and mark your space. Call your spirits and throw yourself into it. You may be planning a small thing or a life-altering thing. It does not matter. What matters is that it is an honest thing. Earnestness will invoke a power far greater than what comes in fancy displays.

And please, know that you are never alone. An entire lineage of ancestral ceremonialists will be calling in the forces of goodness with you.

I will see you on the other side of the gate, for that is where you will be when you are finished.

The Passage

of

Your Ceremony!

Woo-woo!!

PART II

THE LANDSCAPE OF CEREMONY

Initiation into Mystery

Did you do it? Did you do it?

You did it! You've passed through the gate! Woo!

Welcome! The landscape here is different. It is just as profound and intricate as the one we traveled, but now the horizon seems further away, our scope is broader. Isn't that the way things are? Just when we think we've figured things out, everything changes, right?

How was your ceremony, my friend? How did you feel? Was it fun? Awkward? Cathartic? Were you nervous? It was for sure an effort—meaning that energy was expended in the direction of your intention—so I know that something moved. Maybe it was everything you expected.

That's pretty rare. Oh, did I not tell you that? Whoops, well, maybe there wasn't time. Maybe it didn't fit in at the moment. Maybe the trickster fox was acting out, but I can tell you now that there is an element of ceremony that we can never plan for, control or ever really understand. It is the sacred.

When beautiful things happen unexpectedly, it's easy to accept. When things go horribly wrong, not so easy. A friend gets sick and has to cancel. The cat runs out as you leave your house, making you late. Altar items get broken. It is not unusual to be in the middle of a personal ceremony and realize that your intention isn't what you wanted at all, that another more powerful intention has appeared in the course of making sacred space. When a candle sputters or you see a shape in the moonlit clouds that has radical new meaning for you, have fun with it, in a pirates' creed sort of way:

"Make a plan. Carry forth the plan. Throw away the plan. Charge!"

And then hold space for whatever happens. Consider the following story.

One night during a ceremony, a man accidentally dropped the wrong bundle of papers into his sacred fire. Horrified, he scrambled to retrieve them, but it was too late. Then he considered what was burning before him. They were plans he had drawn for a house that would overlook his favorite creek, on the family property. He had made them years ago, but it was an old dream that could never be. The land had been sold. As the man watched his dream turn to ash, he felt, despite his anguish, a sense of relief for not having to carry it anymore. His spirit lightened. The next day he noticed a further lightness in his step, and to his surprise, he started envisioning a new dream. This dream blossomed, and by the end of the year, he moved away from his hometown to another part of the country. There, he felt more at home than he had in many, many years.

You have been given a template for effective ceremony, but you never know where it will take you. Thanks for taking the risk and stepping into the mysteries. Your seed has blossomed! Now your body knows what it feels like to travel the terrain of the sacred.

Keep this template in your heart as an architect keeps her slide rule nearby. Trust it, as well as your instincts, and you will learn to fly—or swim depending upon your fancy. All ceremony, no matter how small, is inherently special and you, as a human, are a natural.

Remember that mastery of any discipline starts with fluency in the basics. Then, we move into realms where we use what we have learned to go even further. We are able to bend the rules while still adhering to their underlying principles. Sometimes, we blend the principles and come up with something new. At that point, we have become contributors to the practice.

Your Personal Practice

Now you are ready to build your personal practice. When ceremony becomes a way of life, your experiences are recorded as your own personal epic of ever-advancing, spiral transformation. A store of knowledge and wisdom is built, providing tools for times of crisis, and lasting nourishment when times are fallow.

Private ceremony has special benefits that cannot be experienced when other people are around. It is a time when you can be raw, completely honest with yourself and your emotions. You can be open and curious like a child in the playroom, an artist tinkering in her studio or a baker in his kitchen, feeling completely alone in a good way. You may notice that your inner light is stronger, because there is no one to lean on. The effort feels louder, more vital. In the sanctuary of your home, you can begin a sacred endeavor and then continue it over the course of many weeks. Your intentions can be multiple and interwoven, and since you are the only person who has to keep track of them, you can spontaneously respond when the unexpected arises.

Ahhh. Relax. You can finally give attention to aspects of your life that have been overlooked! You can answer those voices that call out to you when you are worrying through the morning commute, the groceries, the job. Maybe a voice is telling you that you lose power when you go right to the computer before greeting the day. Maybe it's time to let a destructive friendship go. Maybe your home feels stale, and it's time to do a house clearing and blessing.

If what's up for you is big, like a crisis or life-changing event, self-care may still mean inviting loved ones to witness your ceremony and support your process. We are not meant to go through these things alone. If they agree to come, be sure to tell them what their role is, so they can settle in and you don't have to take care of them.

If you have trouble getting a ceremony off the ground because something feels off, it's probably because you haven't made your space private enough, or you are too concerned about details, or you are not allowing yourself to be vulnerable and express yourself. It's important that you don't cut corners in creating a private, safe, undisturbed sanctuary. You need to be somewhere you will not be called upon and where there are no witnesses. If a loved one in the next room can hear you talking out loud or drumming, it is not private enough. If you don't have this in your home, maybe you can find another place.

A lot of times, we just feel yucky and need to find out why in order to know what to do. You could use the whole first section of your ceremony to discover this through meditation or divination. Sometimes I throw down a few tarot cards and, through the reading, find a place in my life that needs shifting. Then a ceremony comes to me. I move from the kitchen to the living room, figure out the details and enact it. The cards might stay on the table for days, until I feel their energy dissipate.

Every few years, I like to set candles on my kitchen table to create sacred space, and then vision a new life by drawing with my colored pencils. It might take hours or days. I hang the finished drawing on the wall and ponder it for many months. I am not skilled at drawing, by the way, but it means something to me. I look at my scrawl, and there I am on the paper—my energy, my feeling. There it is, manifested, reminding me of what is important. Sometimes the patterns I see in the drawing give me clues as to a ceremony I can do to help manifest the vision. I might find that there is an area that needs expansion through a new drawing. When the energy from the drawing wanes, I take it down.

Personally, I tend to *find* myself in private ceremony more than I plan it. I wake up too early in the morning and there is a rustle in the trees, calling me out of bed, out of the house, into the car, down to the water, and there is the sunrise. My spirits know what I need. They call to me when I forget to spend time with them. The profound beauty of the morning opens me, and I am a hair's breadth away from the sacred. The patterns of color and mist on the water speak to me, reflecting back my difficult emotions, showing me how they can flow towards health. I take all this inspiration back home and do a ceremony. While I prepare, I look at the sacred items I have around my home and ask, "Who wants to come?" I gather them together and interpret how they relate to my need. From that, much of my ceremony is created.

I open my circles with nonverbal invitations to my helping spirits. I dance. I observe what is inside me, and then I hush my mind in order to focus on my inner temple, my jewel, my light, my body. I breathe, and I move again, feeling the difference. My mind slows. My relationship with myself and my spirit friends is reaffirmed. I give thanks for the steadying and open my circle. In my new state, my problems appear smaller, and I am further inspired.

Home ceremony is woven into the pattern of my life. I am not that disciplined, so instead of establishing a routine, I keep my ears open for the call and try to be present when the time is ripe. The moon sings to me from outside the window. The spirits tug at my mind, asking me to do a spirit journey and visit them. When I am cleaning, I find items that can't be thrown away without a little attention. If I don't have the time to respond in the moment, these things get put on my 'to do' list, right along with the groceries, and they stay there until they are done.

I rarely miss a Sabbat (Equinoxes, Solstices and the cross-quarters in between), but that is all the structure I have.

In order for you to have a personal practice, you might need to schedule it. We all have different ways of working. What is important is that you feel a flow happening in your life, and that when things start to feel stagnant, confused or blocked, you take the time to do ceremony and get things moving again.

In this time when so many people have rejected formal religions, ceremony is becoming ever more intimate and personal. We might start off using traditions, books and other people's ideas for inspiration, but at some point, we move into making our own. Years later, we look back and notice themes, complimenting and contrasting, coming together to form our own colorful, personal tradition.

For instance, I noticed that I have a habit of putting little two-to-four-inch mirrors on shelves, tables and altars to make them more sacred. I didn't plan this. It just sort of happened. When I sit down and think about it, I realize that I use mirrors for lots of things. I invoke the element of water with them because they feel like small lakes to me. I use them for protection, resting them outwards against the windows, tipped down to redirect unwelcome energies to the earth. I notice that mirrors also create portals, and carry a sense of the sacred, just like candles do.

No one taught me these things. They just came to me. You will discover your ways, too. Perhaps you are a seamstress, and you find yourself designing altar cloths for specific purposes, carefully choosing just the right colors. Maybe you love to cook, so you whip up special items imbued with your intentions, to be eaten in ceremony. Your magic flows naturally into the activities that you love. It makes you feel more like yourself, and the sweetness of being you becomes your teacher. I wish I could be there and celebrate with you when you find and express your ways.

Blessings on your sanctuary.

May the temple of you
be sovereign,
glowing in the light of
your wisdom.

May you remember your song.

Your Ways

Let us lie under the maple trees and gaze through their branches.

Some days, I feel like all of wisdom is stored in their intricate patterns.

Sometimes, I close my eyes, ask a question and then open them again to find an answer in a particular bend of the tree, or the way a cluster of leaves sways in the wind. I don't know if everyone does this, but it is one of my ways, which have gathered over the years.

What are your ways? What opens you to the sacred? What worked really well in your ceremony? Was it how you created your space? Was it in the beauty of your bridge? If you had your own room as a child, or a nook you called your own, what did you do to make it special? Did you keep a secret collection box under your bed? What sorts of things were in it? What did they give you?

After the revelations of ceremony, it is good to take time to digest. It makes room for more in our feast of life.

We are spending the night here with the maples, before going down to the ocean.

THE HOLLOW BONE: BRINGING YOUR CEREMONIES TO THE WORLD

The magic of our journey stretches and shortens time. We have come down from the mountains, through the foothills and reached the beach in one morning. Peer through the high grass, and watch the white foam crest the waves. This is a place where countless public ceremonies have been held, a place of stories and playful mishaps.

The Hollow Bone sings, "Open. Open." It calls us to open ourselves in service to others. It doesn't ask us for gifts we don't have. It only asks that we share what is already in us, the magic we discover in our personal practice. If your gifts support public ceremony in any way, it is only you who can bring that to us. No one has the same exact gifts to give.

If you are called to bring ceremony itself back to our public arena, this is a profound community service you are stepping into. You will be filled with the fires of inspiration, and you will weep with the beauty you witness. You will be challenged, and you will be blessed with the unique contributions of many people. You are stepping into a current of energy that many have entered before you.

You are so greatly needed, my friend. I don't know why, but, much to my disquiet, I have found that it is a rare person who is called to do this work. At the same time, not all who are called can stay humble enough to be effective. The Hollow Bone teaches us that the power of ceremony comes through us, and then, filled with inspiration, we turn to others and pass the power to them. We hold the container for them through the planning process, treating it as sacred in its own right. We enact together, time and time again, and we are woven into a tapestry of life-affirming experiences. As we keep our vision in this collective weaving, we stay in tune with the work that needs to be done, the songs that need to be sung.

In public ceremony, we are able to draw bigger, collective power into our circles. We witness each other, and we learn from each other. The role of a ceremony leader, in some ways, is to bring the broader forces back into balance. This could mean recovering a peaceful balance in our hearts. It could mean guiding a community back into harmony with its own values. It could mean calling us all into cadence with the natural cycles of death and growth in order for us to let go of the past and live fully.

There are many elements to this artful practice, from managing people and logistics, to the sacred work of listening to spirit and taking care of oneself in the process. Most of us are good at some of these things and not so good at others. These skills, I am sure, you will grow into with each ceremony you bring forth for your community. Most of all, I hope you find others who carry the skills you do not have, so that you can work together in partnership.

As we travel through this next passage, I will sing to you my song of the Hollow Bone. While we rattle again the Bones of Ceremony, I will tell you stories of my times with the most precious people. Later, when you venture into this landscape on your own, you may be tending the needs of entirely different communities; the Hollow Bone will teach you the right songs for them. For now, may the pearls of wisdom I found in my time be of assistance.

Intention & Crafting

The Heart of Community

When we are planning a public ceremony, we need to know what the community needs, so we put our ear to the ground and listen for common songs of yearning. We initiate conversations, hold meetings and read community forums. We also can intuit what seems to be missing in our shared dynamic. For instance, if the group conversation has been overly-cerebral, too caught up in urban life, people may have become collectively disengaged. Then, a Spirit of the Land ceremony might be refreshing for everyone. Sometimes, the need is smack in the middle of the news and social media.

As we listen to the stories of need and come to understand them, we eventually distill them into a statement of ceremonial intent. Ask people what their ideas are, and then mirror them to others.

"Hey, I heard some people say it would be great to do X. What do you think of that?"

They might present a different idea than what you just said, or help shape the original idea a little more. Then you take that new idea and go talking about it to some more people. You're like a human bulletin board. Eventually, everyone will be talking about it, and there will be a song rising up you cannot deny, the collective need revealing itself, a nerve in the community. Hit this nerve in your ceremony intention, and you will see a lot of people show up.

At the same time, as an organizer, your labor of love is going to be most powerful if you are working on a cause that you yourself are passionate about. So, find the cause that serves both you and your community. It won't be too hard.

Try to be aware of what other groups in town are doing, to avoid repetitive themes and conflicting dates. I remember one spring, I attended three events that had us start off as a seed on the floor and then grow into the dance of a plant. I was so tired of being a seed after I burst my pod in the first ceremony, I couldn't connect with the concept anymore!

When the intention of the ceremony is set, it will need to be communicated to everyone who is participating or who might participate, as much as is humanly possible. It goes on the flyer. It will be stated at the beginning of the ceremony and stated in the middle as well.

You might want to do the ceremony-crafting yourself because of a lack of resources, or you might be able to include a few more people. When you do, be sure that you have at least one tangible way that attendees can contribute their personal prayers. Perhaps they can add something to the fire or release something in the water—there are many ways. Public rituals run the risk of being alienating without this crucial part.

Don't turn your ceremony into a performance. I believe that public ceremonies performed by a few while everyone else watches are disempowering. There are some communities that perform closed ceremonies which require highly specialized roles, where you might see one person up on a platform or a group of people enacting a mythological story. It looks like a performance, but it isn't. The attendees have come with a common understanding as to what metaphysics are being practiced, and they know how to energetically support the people in these roles. In open, public ceremonies, there is no time to give much explanation beyond what the main intention is and how participants can take part. When people come from many different backgrounds, finding a common spiritual language to explain what is going on with an advanced ceremony typically isn't worth the effort. You might lose people and the long explanation could create performance anxiety, sending people out of their bodies and into their heads.

Here is a hypothetical example of navigating the process of creating public ceremony. There is a local café where a man shot multiple people, killing a few well-known regulars, sending others to the hospital. People are distraught, isolated in their grief, which is being expressed in many ways. The atmosphere at the café is still charged with violence and fear. Underlying this is emptiness, a community need for a mourning ceremony.

In order to get to a consensus on intentions, I invite everyone who is deeply affected to a planning meeting. At the meeting, I state that we are there to plan a mourning ceremony, but that we need to get more specific about what we will be doing. Then I ask everyone to take a moment of silence to get clear on what their hearts yearn for. Why did they come? Where do they feel the power is for them? We do this without regard as to how to meet their need, or whether it would even be possible. Dreams are not hindered. Personal needs often resonate with community needs, so we want to hear them all.

Then we go around and lay each individual need on the table to see how they all fit together. We discover common themes, what is crucial for some, and the less important things that might be willingly removed. I don't let anyone take something off the table they are passionate about just because it doesn't seem to fit.

For example, one person wants to offer catharsis through community sharing. Another wants a time of silent, non-denominational prayer for the souls of the dead. A third person wants to restore the spirit of the café to a sense of wholeness again. Then someone comes in late. He is enraged by the shooting. He wants to channel the ceremony efforts into a campaign against gun violence. We don't make any decisions. Instead, we fully listen to everyone's needs. Revelations always come.

The Bone of Intention

Next comes the weaving part. I try to approach it with a sense of creativity and lightness in order to encourage people to join in. When we look at all the ideas, in some ways they seem to conflict. Silence. Talking. Space Clearing. Advocacy. But when we look at them another way, they complement each other. Sending love to the souls of the dead could help them cross over, and as a result, they won't be hanging around the café anymore. Allowing people to speak, especially at the location of the shooting, changes the energy of the café. Then there could be another activity to bring in new energy.

Let's say that there was a disagreement about whether to include political advocacy at the mourning. In order to allow people to grieve without conflict, the committee agrees to have an information table about gun violence, but there will be no speeches about the issue. Whoever facilitates the ceremony will make a statement that all forms of grieving are acceptable and point to advocacy as one of those expressions.

It looks like all of these intentions fit together, after all.

Someone has brought a book they love and wants to use a ceremony or poem from it and… it doesn't feel quite right. I ask them to hang on until our intentions are clear, and then I go back to them and ask them what exactly about the poem or prescribed ceremony resonates with their personal need. If this person is on fire, there may be something important there for us, so I need to find out what that it is and honor it.

When individual intentions don't seem to work together, I ask people to explain their thinking more clearly. For some magical reason, whether it is the care and the listening, or some wild, unconventional idea that brings it all together, it always works out.

Once the general intentions are set, I read them back to everyone to make sure we are all on the same page.

> We want to offer a space for community grieving, as well as prayers and support for the dead. We want to encourage new life, which we feel will already have begun with the first two intentions. Lastly, we want to offer a way to change the situation that caused this horrible event to happen.

The Bridging Bone

It's really hard to keep ideas about props, music and color from rushing in as intentions start to crystallize, so I'm not too strict about it. I don't want to block people's creativity. Sometimes, the pieces of the ceremony come together simultaneously. After you've had some practice, you'll be able to catch them all and make sure that expression aligns with intention as you weave.

For the public mourning, the planning group has decided to ask everyone to wear colors that represent life to them. Everyone meets in the park across the street from the café. Wooden dowels with multi-colored ribbons are passed around. As a brass band leads the parade towards the café, the ribbons are waved, creating a colorful scene and fueling a community boost of energy.

The people reach the café and march right inside. The horns blast the whole space with everyone crowded in there, and the band does a finale. Then a spokesperson welcomes everyone and states the reasons for the gathering. They point out that a small, inspired team has set up a side area as an altar to the dead, representing the many different cultures of the people affected. There is paper for people to write prayers and blessings for the dead, which will be burned at the end, out in the parking lot. The chef is serving the favorite desserts of the deceased for everyone to share.

Then the open mic begins, which could be words or songs from the musicians in the community. Some inside jokes from the café regular community are shared in the form of a large banner. Donations are gathered for the mourning families and for the construction of a new stage in the café.

Finally, the written prayers and blessings are brought outside. Someone leads a guided meditation that helps people visualize sending love to the souls of the dead. The prayers are burned. Someone plays a flute and then the ceremony ends in a long, shared silence. People are welcome to stay and socialize.

Notice that for a huge and complicated theme like grief, many ways have been offered for people to express themselves. This meets the variety of emotions felt in the community. It makes everyone feel included, more safe to be themselves, and as a result, the ceremony's healing capacity is enhanced.

There seems to be a direct relationship between how many people attend a ceremony and how complex the intentions can be without creating confusion. In public ceremony, it is more effective to keep the intentions and actions simple and generic, and not to change them. Simple, so that you don't have to explain yourself fifty times, and generic so that each person can find a private intention that still fits the general bill. For example, if you are celebrating Winter Solstice, you don't want to tell everyone to make resolutions. Not everyone considers solstice the new year. A generic representation of the coming of light will work just fine.

In smaller groups, intentions can be more specific, because there are fewer people to agree. Even when we cannot agree, we can still create space together around a broader theme and then have the culmination of the ceremony be a time for individual work, followed by mutual sharing and closing.

It is natural for people to lose sight of ceremony intention in their excitement to find marvelous props. Say someone has fifty green candles they want to donate, but you don't know how green relates to your ceremony. Another person wants to leap over a fire, but it's not clear why. You want to steer them back, but you don't want to wind up sounding like the energy police and taking all the fun out of it. The energy loss from that is going to be far more costly than the misdirected use of a well-loved symbol.

I remember once when I was guiding a ceremony design process, I noticed that someone in the group became offended when I asked him how his suggestion served our intention. I said, "Look, I don't care if you want to have a five-foot, blow-up, green Gumby in our ceremony, as long as you can convince me that it serves our intention."

This caused a chuckle and opened up the gates of creativity for a lot of people. If you don't know you're making lasagna before you start cooking, you might end up with an egg noodle scramble.

For another example, let's use the first Rain Ceremony offered by the Turtle Spirit Jam. Turtle Spirit Jam was a circle in Seattle that I founded and facilitated for almost nine years. It started off as a drum circle with a wee bit of ceremony, but over the years, it blossomed into a full, nondenominational drum, dance and song ceremony with many volunteers and a handful of rotating facilitators. For this particular event, I came up with the original ceremony idea, but my co-facilitator, who was versed in chemistry, was inspired to add something special.

We wanted to bring people together to celebrate the beginning of the rain season because we live in the Pacific Northwest and our rain season is big. Instead of spending the winter stressing about the weather, we wanted to be in harmony with it. What was the intention? Well, on a community level, the intention was just that, to help bring people into sync with the seasons and also to have the ceremony serve as a teaching.

It was going to be a devotional ceremony, where the act of expressing devotion inspires gratitude from the object of our devotion, thus creating a wonderful loop of contagious love. This is a nice healing for everyone involved, the receivers of devotion as well as the devotees.

We decided that the best way to offer thanks and blessings to the environment would be to raise our energy with improvised music, dance and song inspired by the natural world. What would cedar sound like if it could play our instruments? How about Douglas Fir? Then we'd move on to oak, ferns, the creek... eventually opening the circle to people's suggestions.

Then my co-facilitator said, "Let's have a cauldron of water and put a small fire underneath it."

I thought to myself, "Oh no. He wants to boil the rain? Isn't that torture?" But when I asked further, I found out that in his chemist mind, he had come up with a really great idea.

He said, "There can be a cauldron filled with water set up over low fire so the water will not boil. The steam goes up with our prayers and comes back down later as rain to nourish and bless the land."

Wow. My head exploded. Think of the natural cycles, the interconnectedness of nature. Think of the blessing repercussions. We asked people to gather rainwater in the weeks before the ceremony and bring it to our cauldron so that we'd be honoring the land locally, without using fluorinated tap water. In that way, we'd also honor the land around people's homes. I brought my home-grown lavender so people could blow their prayers on it and offer it to the water. People brought personal items and flowers from their gardens to place around the cauldron as a symbol of their love. Some wore blue to represent water or green to represent the lush trees. Then, we played. The cedar music was so sweetly cedar! I wish I could describe it. Then, with the call of the Douglas Fir, the music shifted. I think someone called out "Squirrel!" and that made everyone silly, and so we had another adventure before we moved on. The spirit jam was truly special.

As a final example, I'll tell you about how the annual Ocean Healing Ceremony with the Turtle Spirit Jam came to be. It didn't take a lot to figure out that people needed a way to express their prayers for Mother Ocean after British Petroleum spilled 3.29 million gallons of oil into the Gulf of Mexico in 2010. Hearts were bursting with sorrow, rage, and a desire to act. I hit a nerve with the ceremony intention so we had a huge attendance, which stuck with us as the years rolled on.

At these ceremonies, new people would come to our area in the park, a little late, looking shy. Our designated welcomers would greet each one of them and hand them a cup. They were invited to walk in the sand to the edge of the sound, fill their cup with water and bring it back to our altar. There, they could pour the water into a large bowl dug in the sand, which was actually an empty fire pit. It was explained that we would be infusing the water with our love and devotion through our music, dance and song.

At the end of the day, when we had exhausted our energy and the water was steeped in our love, we planned to pour it back into the sound.

People were so happy to have something powerful and integral to do! They didn't have to know anybody. They could take a back seat, enjoying the atmosphere and the songs, and still be intimately connected to the work. Soon, water was overflowing into the sand, and we just let it continue, as all that love was finding its way to Mama Ocean anyways.

The Announcement

Once your ceremony is crafted, you have the opportunity to bridge-build in your broader community. Take a look at your plan and ask yourself if there are sections or elements that would be best handled by an outside talent. For example, I wanted to have a strong drum circle but knew that if I had to help the drummers keep the beat down, I wouldn't be able to do my job. I invited a couple of local, female African drum teachers, and they were thrilled. They were not practiced ceremonialists, but they were skilled in the ability to read and ride energy through music.

Contact these people early in your process, before your flyers go out. This allows them to give input that may change your core logistics. If their presence is crucial, make sure you align your schedules. Engage in this kind of bridge-building and cross-cultural pollination, and you start hearing exclamations of joy as people run into each at different events. This is community, yes!

The flyer/social media posting is your first sacred invocation of the ceremony. It is *the* call to community to come and gather, so you want to get it right. It states the purpose, place, how people can get involved and what they should bring. It is a highly potent, spiritual document, so try to make it reflect the energy you are attracting. Not everyone will bring items you request, but some will. As the saying goes, the more someone puts in, the more they will get out, and you want to give them that opportunity. Put it out about six weeks in advance and then again six days before the event. Social media boosts can happen one or two days before.

When you make your call, ask for help! Do this not only in the flyer but by personally contacting people whom you know will be valuable. Ask people who love this event and are connected to other communities to spread the word, even if they personally cannot come. Let everyone know how much they are appreciated. Let them know several times. People need to be told they are important. They love to help make something big and awesome happen. This powerful work of connecting people before the event is your way of sharing power with others, making our webs stronger. It will also prevent you from burning out on your seventh ritual.

Make your ceremonies free. There is a time for classes, workshops and healing clients, and there is a time for play. In our society where isolation is getting deeper and deeper, driving people into their living rooms, we are gravely lacking in ways to gather. There are a lot of people who cannot afford classes and more who think they cannot afford classes because they have not experienced the good medicine of what they are missing.

So please, give. Don't make it a promotional event. Just give. It will come back in ways you cannot guess. If you have to charge to cover the rent, or you are the only organizer and you are pouring hours into it, charge something minimal and make it clear on your flyer that no one is turned away for lack of funds. Talk about how pitching in is what is making these events happen. People love the thought of a barn-raising. If there will be food, make it a potluck and ask volunteers to bring utensils that are compostable or made from recycled materials.

You are creating a temporary, autonomous zone where people can share a powerful experience, make new friends and feel like they are part of something again. This is more valuable than apple pie. This is hot apple pie with hand-whipped cream and a sloppy hug from somebody's grandmother. Do it.

Pre-Ceremony Rushes

The Bone of Passion

When I am ramping up to public ceremony, it seems like I become a conduit for the whole thing. I feel the energy. I have strong intuitions about the shape of things. I can't sleep. I wake up with new inspirations and reach for my pen. I become possessed with the spirit of the ceremony. It builds – and then a few days before the event, it falls out of me, and I know that it's no longer mine. It's with the spirits and those who have marked their course to meet up with us. It is out of my control.

The last day before a big ceremony, I always feel dread, like climbing-under-a-rock-with-a-book-or-getting-into-my-car-and-going-on-a-road-trip-far-away dread. After all this work and excitement, ceremony is the last thing I want to do. It's become a joke between me and my friends. You might feel all kinds of things too, the day before the ceremony: a little excitement, nervousness, temporary insanity. Let the power build on the other side, and don't feel like you have to do anything.

On the day of, right before the ceremony, there is a boost. It creeps in, it builds, and then it builds fast. Anyone who has been a performer or had to speak in public knows this. Some call it stage fright, but most of the time it's just energy rushing into your body to be spent during the event. We humans, we are natural mediums, and the spirits of kindness, they want to help. They get really excited about ceremony and come zooming over. Sometimes we have visions that tell us to change something at the last minute, or we get an inspiration to embellish our plan with final touches. For me, my conceptual brain opens up so much, it can be difficult for me to speak. I have to prepare a cheat-sheet of what I'm going to say, and stick it in my back pocket in case I find myself frozen in front of a room full of people. So, don't worry about pre-ceremony insanity. All you need to do is trust the process. You are already in the flow, so just let go, keep moving and after a while, you will forget those feelings.

Plan to get to the ceremony early and call in the circle by yourself or with a few friends. This extra layer of care is needed because you can't control how the public opening of sacred space will go, and you want to be sure that the sacred container is solid. You are also asking for blessings on the overall ceremony at this time, and for assistance in running it smoothly.

People who have volunteered to set up an altar will be there. Having a strong, well-loved altar roots the whole space and gives everyone a focal point. This is an area that doesn't take a lot of skill but does take a lot of time, so it's better to let someone else do it. All you need is some sort of surface—a table, a cloth, a drawing in the sand with areas reserved for community items—and it will look beautiful.

You will discover that key people are late, even when you asked them not to be. Get over it. Trust the spirits and the ceremony body itself that everything is going to fall into place. You have enough to do yourself right now, getting ready.

Around this time, people who did not RSVP are going to show up and ask if you need help. Be ready for this and have jobs for them. Never turn someone away who wants to help. If someone is asking, they are offering their personal energy towards making the event strong. They are asking to be included. Even more, this person may be about to meet a great friend by volunteering for you. The more the merrier, they say. Have small jobs and big jobs so no one feels overwhelmed or unneeded. During this setup time, don't forget to find a few people who are willing to stay and clean up. Crucial. It's a real bummer when everyone leaves, and you are left with an hour of work all by yourself.

Launching the Ceremony

The Compass Bone

Along with the act of drawing the circle, we establish our space by getting acclimated to each other, remembering why we came and how the ceremony will work. And here's something strange I discovered. People need to hear you, the organizer, speak before the ceremony begins. It doesn't matter how much you want to empower them to call in the circle without your guidance; people naturally look to a leader. I used to feel bewildered by this and wonder why the regulars couldn't orchestrate a powerful opening by themselves, but then I realized that I am just a focal point for people to work off of. I can serve that role for them and keep inviting them to step into their power at the same time.

It was time to begin. Not on the clock, but the air felt very ready, and everyone knew it. I thought I'd do one more thing though.

I said, "Go ahead and call in the directions. We can hold sacred space a bit longer so others can get here."

They didn't need me. I didn't want to grandstand. My head was down, arranging something or looking in my bag. I looked up and saw everyone standing in a circle, waiting for me.

"Oh crap," I thought. "Really?"

"Really," the power said. So, I went over and led them through a sacred opening, and everyone fell into the rhythm of ceremony.

First, I welcome everyone and give credit for people's work. Then, on the precipice of launching in, I stop, smile and ask everyone to introduce themselves to the person next to them and tell them why they came. Lots of people go to these things alone, and I have found this ice-breaker is so welcome, that often I have to merrily reel them in again to get started. It's fun.

I tell them why we are here and state the intention clearly because inevitably a lot of people didn't read the flyer. I explain what the culmination point of the ceremony will be and how people can engage. For example, are there slips of paper for people to write on? What are they for? Where do they go? I introduce the people who are serving the group in various ways so we all know where to get help. Then, I set out some general ceremony guidelines.

I have a 'no spectators' rule with ceremony. Bystanders tend to drain the energy and make people feel self-conscious because they are energetically removed from the ceremony. Witnesses are full participants in every part of the ceremony. They hold loving space for other people, helping them to be strong. Witnessing can be under-rated, so I spend time explaining the power of witnessing before we begin. When everyone knows their job, it cuts down on the shuffling noises in the back.

As I mentioned before, I cannot do this without a cheat sheet. It doesn't matter if every detail of every aspect of what we are about to do is imprinted in my bones, when I am in front of a crowd of people, the bottom of my brain just falls out, leaving me senselessly muttering. Then I go into this moment of insanity where I truly believe that it is more important that I *don't* fully describe everything so people can fill in the creative gaps themselves. Then I walk away, and people don't know what we are doing. Do yourself a favor. Make a cheat sheet of what you need to cover. A short bullet point list works best so you are not reading long paragraphs and getting lost in all those words. Better to face your people and talk to them so they can see your eyes.

After telling you all that, I suggest keeping the opening relatively short so the energy that has been building doesn't start going back down. There is no way to cover everything. To do that would be a workshop in itself, right? So, choose the things that seem important for that day and that group of people. Another joke that has gone around with my organizers is that it seems like the one thing I neglect to mention is always the one thing that we inevitably will run right into during the ceremony. Such is the spectacular adventure of controlled chaos.

Invocation

The White Bone of Sacred Space

When you do invocations for an open public ceremony, use generic spiritual language. This goes for the promotional materials, as well. We are in the midst of a spiritual renaissance, so your audience will likely represent new and old spiritual practices from all over the world. We don't want to describe a cosmology that someone cannot engage with because it doesn't fit their personal practice. As for those who don't have a practice, be aware that some may have a strong resistance to being told how things are in the spiritual realms. Many people are still running, wounded, from organized religions, and it is common for them to resist committing to any one path. I want to leave doors open for everyone to engage.

I don't even name specific spirits when I call in the directions in public. I have everyone face the directions with me, and I play music or sing. I may comment on how the sun sets in the West, on the home of the ocean peoples we are gazing at, because that is something undoubtedly beautiful that we can all agree is true. I invite others to simultaneously practice whatever they are used to. I may state that inviting Jesus, or other deities who are sometimes shunned by alternative cultures, is welcome. Most of the time, people are shy, but it's nice when someone takes a twirl or sings their sacred song. Don't worry about group inhibition. Focus on saying the right things to make people feel welcome and safe. The more time a community has spent together, the more you will be able to ask of them. Then, they will be more liable to get silly and growl like bears, or chant to the rain, or dance in the dew. In the meantime, just build some extra energy-raising activities into the ceremony.

After all this, try to let go. Have a strong beginning and then get out of the way. Allow people to make mistakes, enjoy the mishaps, disappear into the crowd if your presence is making people follow only you. Love people through all of it. Introduce yourself to new folks and make them feel welcome.

And last but not least, enjoy yourself. Spend a few minutes with your friends. If you didn't get enough volunteers to cover all the bases, let things slide so you can get a hug or two. Take the time to eat something, and don't let yourself get dehydrated. Ask for help if something needs immediate attention. See how much they can do without you.

Tending the Sacred Container

When people go into trance, it's easy for them to lose sight of the ceremony intention. So we need to talk about how to tend the sacred container and preserve our focus. In large ceremonies, one person cannot do this alone and have a remotely good time. It calls for teamwork. Choose individuals ahead of time to keep an eye out, communicate with each other and help keep everyone safe. Sometimes, the watchers are publicly identified, so if someone runs into difficult emotions during the ceremony, they know where to go to for help. In a musical ceremony, if you don't have designated drummers who are responsible for keeping everyone on beat, listen to the drummers warm up and recruit one or two on the spot.

There are all sorts of things that might wobble or deplete the container. For example, a group of people chit-chatting during invocations creates a huge energy leak. While we are starting to move into the spirit realms, they are pulling us back by keeping their corner in the mundane. Not to mention the distraction. This is really common and easy to solve with a gentle word.

Sometimes a person is so deep in trance, they are not looking where they are dancing. A helpful hand to lead them away from the altar, or from people seated on the floor, can nudge them back into awareness even as they continue their work.

Catharsis and Unexpected Expression

During the peak of a ceremony, someone might lose track of themselves and start emoting intensely, releasing heavy energies. This person might be perfectly fine processing on their own. They might be in trouble and need help. They also might be distracting or hurting the group with their own personal catharsis. How to help them and whether to intervene depends upon the group's intention and capabilities.

When people are in catharsis, they are releasing energy they have been carrying around for a long time. On the spiritual plane, this energy might wind up in someone else's body because that person is in a trance and has their field open. Not a lot of people know how to shield themselves and do their work at the same time.

So, for an event that is open to anyone off the street and isn't meant to be cathartic, I would advise keeping cathartic behavior to a minimum. If the ceremony *is* meant to go deep, I publicly address potential issues. I ask everyone to please remember that we don't have the resources to help them if they go into a difficult place. It's ok to cry. It's ok to have a hard time, but to please remove themselves from the center of the circle if they are not able to stay with the group sync.

Never jump to approach someone in sacred space just because they are crying or look upset, because we don't want to disturb their process. Instead, we assume that they are taking care of themselves until it is apparent that they are not, in which case someone may go up and ask them what they need. If they are distracting the group process, they might be asked to move to another room. I've seen people volunteer to sit with the cathartic person, but that may not always work out. First of all, the volunteer is missing out on the ceremony. Also, they may not have the tools to support a cathartic person without interfering or getting pulled into their muddle.

It takes a special setup to hold space for catharsis. Such ceremonies always open with thorough instruction in what is considered acceptable behavior and how to keep the space emotionally safe for everyone. In regularly held groups, there might not be instruction, but instead there will be a requirement that attendees have previously taken some training.

Because the Turtle Spirit Jam was open to everyone and magnified by ninety minutes of music, I asked the spirits of kindness ahead of time to set up an updraft that would pick up difficult energies and bring them out of the circle to a place where they would be transformed. I think this really helped.

If someone is dominating the ceremony with their emotion, speech, music or in any other way, I usually let it ride for a while to see if the person will bring themselves back. It's fine for us all to have our moment, but if it seems that there is no awareness and they aren't picking up my cues, it gets nipped in the bud. With a gentle word, a subtle hand signal or an intentional shift in the music, I have to do it. It doesn't make me popular, but it can prevent the entire group from falling apart. If I don't do it, eventually people stop coming to my events because they don't feel safe or cared for. What is manageable to you may be too much for someone else. I've seen people become afraid when catharsis happens, and I have had people come up to me after an event and tell me that they can't continue with a group that allows someone to take up so much space.

My job is to protect the group, not save the individual. Still, it's tough having to do an intervention during a ceremony. I consider it a last resort. Honestly, if I can't gently solve a problem in the moment, I'd rather have a bumpy ceremony and take someone aside for a chat later, explaining how their activities are affecting others.

Keeping the Circle Grounded

When the energy is building, having a few, seasoned people stay consciously grounded works wonders. It's natural for the groundedness of the circle to weaken during this time, so the more we can keep it down, the more solid a base we will have when it's time to send our intentions. We need to stay alert to what is going on. We don't want the group to go so far out there, that we don't know what shape people will be in when they come back. Not unless we are in a closed group with experienced practitioners.

Keeping the Focus

Usually, the biggest problem that occurs is that the group gets lost and forgets what they're supposed to do. As much as I try to empower everyone to be active ritualists and feel the energy, the group mind will still expect a directive leader. Transitions from one part of the ceremony to the next don't happen unless I make a signal. I do still wait because I can't stand leading the whole thing, but then I make the call. It's best to give the cue nonverbally, but a verbal cue is better than having everything go off track.

One time, an entire ceremony came to a halt because for some reason everyone decided to stop drumming and have lunch. Mystified, I rounded up some of my team and got the rhythm back. Ok, that's extreme, but it happened. Us Seattleites get a little nutso when the sun comes out after so many months under the clouds. I think the fantasy of being on a beach in California had temporarily taken over the reality that we were in ceremony.

Tending the container truly isn't directive. We certainly don't want to micro-manage. Holding a safe container often means holding back, rather than jumping in at a moment's notice to interfere with someone's spiritual work.

Most tending can happen with a silent prayer, a shift in posture, a change in music, a word to a helper. It's great to tend with other people because we don't always have the same perception as to what is going on. During those times when all of us are at a loss, I appeal to my spirits of kindness. I trust them completely. On more than one occasion when I thought we were headed towards disaster, my spirit guides told me to do nothing, and it was fine.

Tending the energy container isn't that difficult, either. We all know how to feel the vibe of a room. Much of the work is done when setting up the sacred space. A strong, focused opening makes a strong container, especially when the community participates. I always ask the group to help in the opening. If I realize midstream that I am the only one doing it, I turn around and make goofy faces at people, telling them we gotta fuel this rocket together or we aren't gonna get anywhere! It's collective sweat that makes this alchemy work! If I did the opening myself, I would be allowing people to take a back seat or worse, a movie seat. We get up, shake our bodies out, make weird noises, say our names out loud, and we all call in the directions together in any way that comes to us. Then we have an undeniable *us*. And when after the ceremony, we come down together, when we break bread and laugh over the stories, this is it. This is the sweetness of community in ceremony. It's life-giving. There is no way I could have done the large ceremonies without help from other facilitators, leaders and silent helpers from other spiritual communities. I am so very grateful for them.

Times to Loosen Up

Usually, we want to keep the sacred container sealed, with no distractions, but there are times when that is the opposite of what we want. Sometimes it's more important to experience community bonding than it is to have the super-stellar purity of an alchemical, magical feat. Sometimes the magic of shared warmth is what we need the most.

I remember once I went to a gathering put on by a local Native American tribe. I was so excited to see a *real* ceremony, to witness secrets of the indigenous! Well, there was a ceremony, but there were also women gossiping on the sidelines the entire time. There were children running through the room. And there were people eating food throughout. I couldn't believe it. I was horrified. I wanted to tell them they were doing it all wrong. And then I was laughing at myself all the way home in the car. I missed it! I was only thinking about me and magic! I didn't feel the warmth of the family care in the room or appreciate the modeling of tradition for the children. What a dummy.

Big, open, community ceremonies are different from closed ceremonies for adults who want only to focus on the work. In the latter, once members start having children, it is unfortunately common for them to feel left behind. Not only do they lose their own community practice, but their children don't get to be exposed to these wonderful traditions as they grow up. Instead of being frustrated that we can't get down to work without distractions, we need to create spaces that are welcoming to families. We can have ceremonies where there is shared childcare, and we can create traditions that include our youth. If nothing else, the symbols will be imprinted on their memories, to teach them as they grow.

The magic will still be strong. It will just be unpredictable and funny and include all the things that unexpectedly happen when a span of generations is present. Who is better at holding space for this than parents? This *holding* ability becomes woven into the fiber of our community. Family memories act as seeds that bloom and bloom again over the years.

So, instead of thinking about one ceremony as being more correct or more powerful than another, think of it as a spectrum. Think about what is needed for the intention you have. Large gatherings are not necessarily watered down. More people-power charges the space and provides opportunities for relationship-building. Small ceremonies, on the other hand, are focused and intimate, with more opportunity for vulnerability to stoke the fires. My hope is that when we humans return to a life of ceremony, we will have ceremonies in our lives to meet both intimate and community needs, and be free of unrealistic expectations to meet them all in a single ceremony.

Mishaps

When we are bringing large numbers of people together to tap into the unknown and blend our worldly reality with the spiritual realms, things are bound to go wrong. Candles get knocked over. Vital tools disappear. People find themselves in tears. Power rushes in and everyone feels it—well, most people. Some people don't feel anything at all, and go off to the side to graze on the snacks that have been reserved for after the ceremony.

If we pay attention to the messages of mishap, we access a whole other level of meaning. Because we carefully set our container to receive only benevolence, mishaps can be interpreted as helpful, no matter how they appear.

It was another Ocean Healing Ceremony, held on the water's edge, at Golden Gardens park. For the first five years, we did this ceremony right smack in the middle of the most populated area. I don't know why. It was a lot of fun. People gave us a wide berth. They stared. Some asked a lot of questions. Some stopped to join us. A few folks told me that just seeing us do our thing restored something that had been missing for them; it gave them inspiration and hope in the world again.

The other regulars and I met in the early afternoon and staked out a spot with a flag so people could find us. Then we spent the next hour or so setting up, helping people find us, guarding people's stuff by the curb while they parked their car, and generally getting really excited. People brought instruments and food. Parents rolled out blankets for their kids. Eventually, we had a ceremonial opening. Then, for much of the day, there was drumming, dancing and singing as we shared space and gathered energy for the culminating moment when we would send our blessings out to the water. This being a long, public and non-denominational ceremony, people came and left as their schedules allowed, and the core of us held a through-line of energy running to the end.

This year was one of our biggest years. There must've been about thirty, forty people around our circle at any given time—a lot, with all the coming and going. The altar was beautifully crafted by one of our leaders. It had all kinds of seashells and sacred items and was full of color. I always ask people to bring things for the altar to strengthen it and connect them to spirit, so there were lots of personal items as well. We had two professional drum facilitators and an elder woman drum teacher who taught us a Yemoja chant before we started. (Yemoja is a Yoruba water Orisha.)

The day was long and eventful. I walked the perimeter of the circle, welcoming people and talking to interested passersby. Nearby, there was a bunch of young men who were intensely curious. They were capoeira dancers, and they were having a good time with each other, having a party. We talked a bit, and they danced in our circle, too. I was friendly, but after a while I told them that we were having a sober event, so it would be better if they didn't join us anymore.

Later, we were right in the middle of one of the highest points of the ceremony. The drumming was fast and loud. One of my super-talented friends was going crazy on the didgeridoo that he'd painted all over with fish. I was pretty close to the center of the circle, which was many people-layers thick, when one of the young capoeira dancers burst in, placed a paper plate with a cooked hot dog right smack on the altar and ran away. His friends laughed and took pictures. I swear it was a dare.

My co-facilitator looked at me in shock. I was a little stunned, too. What should we do? How should we handle it? Is it a desecration of the altar? A breach of sacred space? Should she take it off? She looked at me, and I held my hands out to the altar and started laughing. We all laughed. The hot dog stayed, and the circle kept drumming.

Then, the big moment came. The sun was setting. We all stood up and faced the water to send our love to the ocean. It was packed and loud and fun and full of music. There were people designated to guard the perimeter, and they were literally holding back a line of capoeira dancers, but our hot dog boy slipped through, and he got right in there, right next to me. He looked at me, remembered who I was and got a little scared. With this 'bad kid' repentant grin on his face, he said, "Ohh, can't I stay?"

I smiled and said—or rather shouted in the din—"This is a ceremony to honor mama ocean. We are going to send our love to her right now. You can't be here if you're drunk."

He was clearly drunk.

He shouted back, "Oh, I know about the Ocean Goddess! I was raised in Hawaii! You gotta let me stay. See I can dance!"

and he danced a crazy, beautiful, oceany dance. Of course, I let him stay.

We all hooted, then chanted, then threw out our arms to the water. The drumming stopped, and another great didgeridoo player sent our prayers out with her beautiful song. There was a hush. When the sun set, people actually applauded. Weird, but really great. Wow.

A few years after the hot dog event, we decided to take the Ocean Healing Ceremony to the end of the beach where people wouldn't find us unless they intended to walk down there. We wanted a little more focus, a little more privacy and less of a spectacle. One wasn't better than the other. It was just time.

On the quiet end of the beach, we had an Ocean Healing Ceremony where community members made an eight-foot goddess out of seashells and seaweed with a bowl of water at her womb. One of our amazing leaders, a talented artist, created a huge turtle sculpture, made of bamboo curtain sections. He brought all the parts to the beach, and it was quite the production to assemble. The turtle's head was on one end of the circle, its tail was on the other, and the feet bordered the sides. The body was us, having our ceremony.

Well, halfway through the ceremony, the tide came in. We kind of freaked out, but our artist told us to let it be. Water poured through the turtle's head. It was a sea turtle, after all. Right?

At that moment, the power of the ceremony was palpable. Our well-laid plans didn't matter anymore, because we were so present with each other. Some of us viewed the turtle sculpture as a sacred talisman being offered to the spirit of the ocean, thinking that our message had been sent that way. For others, the turtle and the water were speaking back to us. Everyone gleaned their own meaning from what was happening. It was beautiful.

Blessings from Beyond

Sometimes, we feel a shift in the container. A five-minute downpour happens. A hawk flies over, screaming. The group energy boosts for no apparent reason, or we are held, in a liquid, quiet stasis.

It was a ceremony for the Salish Sea. Ours was one of many coordinated events that were happening the same day, up and down the coast for at least a hundred-mile span. I was in the middle of explaining to our circle that all creatures are sentient and that the sea creatures, through our hearts and our prayers, were aware that we were holding this ceremony.

At that very moment, someone yelled, "Otter!"

I looked, and miraculously there were two otters bobbing up and down in the waves, looking right at us. I knew otters were not uncommon, but I had never seen them in the park, and I sure didn't expect them to show up that very moment. My whole body filled with joy and the gift of it gleamed through my tears. We stood there and thanked each other, us humans and those otters. Later, when the ceremony was over, they came back and made another appearance.

It is true. Our work is always being witnessed by the unseen, which occasionally has something to say or wants to help us in our endeavor.

Closing and Grounding the Ceremony

The Bone of Home

Our intention fulfilled, the energy we've raised has created a miracle. We are still between the worlds. People are in still in trance, so we carefully help them return to their everyday senses. Some people might be so far out there, it's necessary to call them back verbally. This may take some time.

I have found that some people really like to hang onto the metaphysical highs and don't realize they can keep that good stuff while still coming home to their bodies. Grounding is a really big deal. In shamanic cultures, it is said that if you are not in your body, it can be too easy for someone or something else to find a home there. Even with grounding, after a very powerful ceremony, you can feel ecstatic or a residual trance for a day, which is ok, but without grounding, the extra energy can pull us off-balance.

I can get emotionally overloaded and really spacey. Being in the role of ceremony leader, the energy circuit between my body, the spiritual world and the sacred space is pretty big so if that circuit isn't cut, it can wipe me out. I remember one time when I forgot to ground after a major public ceremony. I was buzzed all the next day, and then I remembered.

"Oh, my goodness!"

POW! I grounded back to the spot on the beach, long-distance magic from my living room. Then I slept about ten hours. Later, I heard from people who had been at the event that they hadn't been feeling that great either, until I did the final grounding.

Another time when I forgot, I was able to get into my car and drive back to the location of the ceremony to ground. That is the preferred way.

Guided meditations will include a built-in section to bring people back into their bodies. Core shamanic spirit journeys, that use the drum or rattle to visit the power animals, have a specific rhythmic callback so journeyers know when to return.

For the active ceremonies, when we are about to end and we have said our goodbyes to the spirits, I emphatically state that we are closing and thank everyone for all that they did. We soak in as much of the delicious energy as we need. I tell them that there truly is enough for everyone. We fuse it with our own bones, to heal with, to grow from, to manifest. Then, together we send the rest of it back.

I try to make the closing shorter than the opening so people don't get bored. Also, if I spend too much time thanking the spirits, people might go back into trance.

In the Turtle Spirit Jam, we fell into a tradition of saying "Thank you!" across the circle and answering with "You're welcome! Thank you!" over and over, acknowledging the fact that there is no offering without a receiving. It would go back and forth, and back and forth, until we were all giggling.

We move aside any items that were set up to mark sacred space. We close the portal to the spirit world and shift our senses back to where we are standing. We are finished. What's for dinner?

Need I say anything about potluck? Isn't the sharing of food in our primal nature as well? We celebrate each other. We joke, we laugh, we form relationships, we create more memories. We get even more grounded through the camaraderie. A ceremony that ends with a meal is a ceremony that builds community. You gotta do it.

After your formal closing, as the group starts to disperse, find a little time to energetically close the circle again, by yourself, and ask for a personal clearing from spirit. It doesn't matter if folks are watching. Just be discreet, don't look for attention, and they will give you space. This grounding is just for you.

Then have a happy party in your mind with your spirits of kindness and just receive. Receive the blessings they are bestowing on you for doing this beautiful, important work. Be in the moment. Receive the gratitude of your community. Go home and rest. Dream a new day later.

Spontaneous Ceremony

Once you have the ceremony design process down, it's super-fun to do it with a bunch of strangers on the very day of the ceremony. No planning committee. Everyone is involved.

It's like a card game. In order to make it feasibly fast, you need to set a general intention for the ceremony ahead of time. Put it in the invitation and encourage people to bring any items they are inspired to bring. Tell yourself that the ritual will be designed in no more than an hour, stick to it and have fun.

Let's say you put out a call to co-create a ceremony for Spring Equinox. You all meet in the park and then you tell them the rules of the game as if you are teaching them how to play rummy.

Ask people to call out why they want to celebrate Spring. Tell them it's like throwing their cards on the table. Keep prompting them, one after another while taking diligent notes on every idea, whether it sounds like it fits or not. Let's say one idea is to celebrate the rush of new life. Another idea is that you should be reflective because Equinox is between the poles of light and dark. Let them both stand. Lay them down. Everything gets put on the table. There's no time for a deep process, so don't try to get every single person's voice. Just take what comes.

Then read your notes back to them and ask them how it can all fit together. If no one jumps in, start making suggestions and let people tweak the plan as it develops.

If someone gets all puffed up, with their face about to explode or maybe they look like they need to go to the bathroom, or they have this 'Oh! Oh!' look on their face, then you know. Inspiration! Spirit is coming through!

If things get tough, ask if anyone wants to take their cards off the table or swap them out now that they have seen everyone else's. Don't let anyone take a card off the table if they are just caving. No caving. If the idea is important, you can find a way to fit it in.

Oh, my goodness, it's super-fun! It's a creative process that everyone gets to be part of from beginning to end. People will feel like they did something; they were included, and their contributions were important. Blessings on the lickety-split ceremonial design style!

Our Unique Call

The Hollow Bone calls us when a ceremony is needed for our people. If we accept, we are given a gift of fire so generous, we know it can't be meant for us alone. Accepting and honoring this gift is a lot like falling in love. Our lives gets bigger. Our hearts burst open. We hear things from the other realms to guide us. We have sudden inspirations, and our hopes glow brightly, influencing all who are drawn to our work.

Some of us hear the call but don't believe in it because we think that such things are meant for other people, but trust me, the Hollow Bone always chooses well. Some of us are frightened because we think the fire will consume us and our lives will be out of control, but that power too is in our hands. We are not meant to hurt ourselves or sacrifice what is dear. The Hollow Bone teaches us that the nature of fire is that it cannot be held. It must move, be channeled, be shared.

So, we connect. We let our inspirations flow out into the world and hear them echo back through the lyrical voices of our people, for whenever someone speaks with passion, there is a song. We offer the fire within us as a service to the community. We offer it to the whole.

For those of us who are not called to leadership, we may experience a different call to service. We may feel an urge to cook for the events, to spend precious sacred time creating an altar, to offer our gorgeous live music. Some people are called to support the organizers, to encourage them and pick up on items that are not getting covered.

We have evolved beyond the concept of the charismatic leader, for it no longer serves us. As community members, we must refrain from giving our personal power to single points of light and instead nourish our own talents. We need the people who carry torches to see the many torches. We need them to be responsible and refuse when others try to place them on a pedestal.

A good leader is a sharing leader, one who cannot function without the many hands and minds of the community. A good leader consults with others and fosters their visions. For ceremony is not about power. It is about celebrating and growing together.

Hearing the Call

Look. We've come to a rushing river.

See the waterfall above and feel the cool spray moisten your face. Much has been said. There is much to be pondered.

When have you felt the instinct to let something flow through you that is calling from beyond? What draws you into the magic of transformation? Is it in your tinkering with metal, wood or clay? Is it in the way you hold space for your family? Are you a writer? Do you find clarity in gathering resources for a greater project? Maybe you love making things with your hands. Or do you find joy in creating connections amongst the people you meet? Are you highly attuned to the emotions, the ache of the communities around you, calling to be released into movement? What? What?

Let the rush of water clear your mind and allow yourself to be empty. Feel the pounding of the cascade vibrate in your body, and listen.

Listen.

Where is your place in this web of healing? What is it that you have been called to do? This is your medicine, for when we follow the call, we are always blessed with the gift of creative fire.

THE BONE OF HONOR:
EACH OTHER

An adolescent boy cackles over a black, bubbling cauldron. His face is smudged with soot and his eyebrows burnt.

"I've almost got it this time!" he exclaims. "Now, I'll be a real magician!"

This all too familiar fantasy novel or Hollywood scene has nothing to do with true ceremony. It isn't ceremony at all. It is metaphysical technique taken out of the loving container of ceremony, used for personal gratification and aggrandizement. This incessant seeking of magical power and notoriety has no value in the real world. Our world needs deep understanding of love and relationship. It needs compassion.

In enters an old woman. She removes her cloak and is revealed as the bountiful crone that she is. Her presence is like a mountain, her voice like soothing water, her bearing radiant. Her life experiences are etched across her body in a spiderweb of lines—her trials, her triumphs, her losses and her long journey back to her true self. She is open, yet guarded in her wisdom. She moves and the air moves with her.

The adolescent is silenced. He wants the crone's power, but her power does not come from magic tricks. It comes from walking the long path of service and truth, from enduring dismemberment after dismemberment, from the slow awakening of her body to its connection to all that lives.

There is nothing she can say to transfer her wisdom to him. She can only open a door and point, but likely he will not see it. So, she writes down guidelines to keep him from harming himself or others as he walks his own path, the only one that will truly teach him.

There was a time in history when the precepts of magic were only taught to those who had gone through many trials and could fully understand the gravity of what they were being given. It is true that some teachers did not have the strongest of ethics, but others were careful to teach only students who were good of heart and unlikely to misuse their talents. These days, many practices are still kept within the circles of the adept, but the foundations of working with metaphysics have come out of the box. Manipulation of the metaphysical is only a web search away. While this can be viewed as a great contribution to the collective knowledge of the human race, it can also be viewed as a dangerous development.

At this time in history, we are seeing, in various spiritual subcultures, high numbers of people imbued with psychic powers they did not seek and have no training to handle. Some are able to find support from their elders. Others become overwhelmed as information floods their amplified empathic or psychic senses, causing near or real neurosis. Then there are those who use their untempered abilities and exaggerated charisma to manipulate those around them and fuel their own egos, leaving a path of psychic violence in their wake.

Ceremony is innate to all humans, something anyone can do. However, the ways of using energy, when studied, can go far beyond the everyday cultivation of one's ceremonial skills, or understanding of the sacred cycles and our healing process. This is an arena that is not meant for everyone, not only because it is just not some people's 'thing' but because not everyone has a talent or the commitment or fortitude to handle those advanced levels of knowledge. Yes, it is easy to learn the techniques, but to learn to use them wisely requires arduous journeys into one's own wounds. It is not fun work and requires an undeniable calling. Once you are called, it is impossible to leave the path. I don't know why. It is just the way it is.

So, is it better to keep the ways of magic secret? Or is it better to talk openly about them and help uncross the wires, explain the repercussions and set some guidelines? I have consulted with my own spirits of kindness, and I have chosen both. I hold back some areas of knowledge, and I talk openly about the foundational areas which most people seem to be exploring. I also wrap this entire event of the singing of the ancient bones, this sacred journey, in a spell of protection for the good of all.

Protection Spell of the Slippery Hold

Oh, seeker of the mysteries of ceremony,
may these words find you opening into yourself.

May the ways described in these pages protect you and quench your
thirst for meaning, and may the sun nourish your seedlings.

May your heart's intentions blossom in beautiful manifestation.

May the creative force within you guide you
towards your true vocation.

May you find healing when you call out for help.

May you come to understand the spiraling cycles of living and dying.

And if you intend to use these sacred words to harm,
entrance or bind another,
may they slip between the pages, ungraspable.

May your ceremonies slide across banana peels, with humor,
loss of timing and no harm to anyone.

May your efforts be for naught, finding no traction.

So Mote It Be, According to the Will Placed on My Teachings
and For the Good of All.

- Tasara Ravenheart

The Bone of Honor sings to us of how to treat each other kindly and delicately in the amplified sphere of ceremony.

The Sanctity of Psychic Space

It is easy to understand that sexual assault is an inadmissible violation of body and psyche. In the same way, our psychic space must not be violated. This is because of the universal law that states that we all have sovereignty over our own private sphere. To honor this, we do not send energy into other people's fields without explicit permission, whether it be to harm or to heal. Not implied permission, but explicit permission.

To try to help or heal someone without their permission is interfering with their free will and their sovereignty. We may do it and see what we perceive as good results, but we may not see that we have greatly delayed the other in finding what they truly needed. Some of us warriors are so hard-headed, life has to knock us down a few times before we figure things out. No one can change that for us. If we are prevented from experiencing the very pain that will teach us, we are sentenced to another cycle of agony. No one knows where bottom is for another person. In cases of near death, it is also not our place to keep a soul from crossing over when it is their time and choice.

To harm or bind another being in order to prevent them from hurting others, even if we consider it "tough love," is just that—harmful and binding. It can't be defined in any other way. Also, what we do to others, we do to ourselves. We are so intricately connected to the web of life that our actions, words and thoughts will always be reflected back to us, in ways that are obvious as well as obscure. If we harm someone, we have changed the shape of the most private space inside ourselves. We have shaped our world into one where harming is a go-to, instead of the harder path of seeing through the eyes of love. We have limited the kinds of beings who are willing to interact with us. This is an even more difficult road, one which we cannot return from without a painstaking, arduous journey.

I knew about magic before I knew about the spirits of kindness. When I first met them, they took me on a spirit journey and showed me the harm I had caused with a binding spell. They told me that they would not teach me anything more until I reversed the spell. I witnessed a level of pain I did not know I had inflicted, and it was clear to me that I would never, ever do that sort of magic again. It was a horrible but necessary revelation.

If you cast any sort of predatory magic on another person, you cannot help but bind yourself to them because you have invested your own emotion and energy into changing their lives. Luckily, there are many other ways of dealing with aggressive or dangerous people. We start on the physical plane by simply speaking up. We create boundaries by saying no. If we need help or are worried about the safety of a community, we can let others know what is going on. Energetically, maintaining a solid, loving container (not a feigned one) can transform situations. If we are not capable of this, we need to be honest about it and then turn our focus to our own self-care. We then divest every speck of our energy from the situation and steer clear, physically, emotionally and energetically. We can even remove our energy signature from that person's awareness. It's our energy. We want to keep it for ourselves.

Common psychic space is a different arena from personal psychic space. If a business is going to cast enchantments of greed, over-sexualization, body shame and consumerism into the collective psychic field, I am not going to have any problem with directing the essence of green growth, mutual respect, sharing and kindness into the same field. The collective consciousness is supposed to be a people space, not an institutional space. We have town squares, not the Safeco square or the Pepsi square—oh, yes, the corporations *have* taken over and regulated our town squares, literally. So, we have the right to take them back in the collective consciousness. If we don't, and we let their song of the straight path continue to lure people away from health, we may not survive.

We can flood the collective with our own songs about the world we want to live in, with any music, vision or flavor of healing energy we want. We cannot, however, intend a result that would interfere with other people's free will. We cannot direct energy at individuals, but we can hold out support for people in general. We place our gifts in the common space, and they will be there when others reach for them.

Sometimes it feels like the psychic town square is cluttered, depressed, degrading, violent, filled with loss, loneliness, avarice and despair, but we do not want or need to go to battle with it. Instead, we sing of the sacred spiral in whatever way we know how, and we shine, allowing our beautiful minds to craft and contribute. Don't underestimate the power of your light. It influences those around you, without your even knowing it.

We can send grounding energy into situations that are getting out of hand. We can ask the spirits of kindness to stand by those that are lost with the disclaimer that our intentions will not interfere with their free will. We can pour loving light into the common collective, asking it to go where it is needed and called for.

We don't have to expose ourselves to the crazy town square all the time, just as we don't have to listen to the news all the time. We must take care of ourselves when we do this work. We can connect to the collective web of people doing this work when we do our meditations and visualizations. It is magnificent and nourishing to be in touch with the potential here. When we let fly our ceremonial hope to bring the great forces back into balance, it only makes this goodness stronger.

This is an area where we do not have enough ceremony. There is so much we can do without violating the psychic fields of individuals or tampering with their free will.

The Sanctity of Personal Vision

When someone has a vision in a meditation, or a frog crawls across their foot right before a ceremony, be very, very careful not to interpret the signs they are receiving from the spirit world. Frog might mean silliness to me, but it might mean fly-eater to someone else. Another person may have just read a book about a frog, but the one whose foot has been doused with frog slime just had a childhood memory sparked and now she's thinking about her long-lost brother. If we rush in there and paint a meaning on it for her, we could disturb the revelation unfolding inside her. Also, this frog may have moved her on a level that is so personal, she is afraid to talk about it. So we try to be delicate and allow her to enter the secret world of gentle whispers on her own. If we interfere, she may shut down and not share anything at all, when she might really need to talk.

I don't even comment on people's dreams. If a friend asks me about his dream, I turn it around and ask lots of questions designed to help him pry the meaning out for himself. This is a listening practice, a holding practice, a way of empowering our friends. The only person who really knows what these messages from spirit mean, is the person they were meant for. Even when I go on a spirit journey with my drum and ask my power animals specific questions for my friends, I just report back what the power animals said or did and let the receiver interpret it for themselves.

The Sanctity of Personal Space

When someone becomes emotional in a ceremony, it can be tempting to go over and comfort them, especially if they are your friend. If you are really concerned, just keep an eye out and hang back. It is a gift to be able to have a deep process in a public circle. We don't want to encroach. It might be appropriate to ask them if they need anything or guide them to the side if they are distracting others, but as a general guideline, don't. Do not touch someone having an emotional moment,

especially from behind. This can be very jarring, and for someone with an abuse history (which is most of us), it's the absolutely wrong thing to do. Trust they can handle themselves until it becomes apparent that they cannot.

Even when something amazing, joyful and transformative is going on with someone in ceremony, I tend to look away. I am aware and gauge the effect on the overall dynamic, but I am careful not to gaze too long. I want to grant them energetic privacy as well as physical privacy.

Another boundary regards sacred items. Many people bring things for the altar that have private meaning for them. Some people bring items intending to charge them and take them home for healing. Some people bring items that have already been energetically charged from their personal altars. To touch these items not only interferes with the energy of the item but is not safe for you. If something was placed on the altar to be cleared of sorrow or despair, we don't want to absorb that energy into ourselves. We want to allow the mystery and magic to happen in the altar space without interference.

Musicians have personal relationships with their instruments, and many do not share them with anyone. Some instruments are even considered sacred. If you want to play something that is not yours or even touch it, find out who owns it and ask. If you are hosting a sacred jam with lots of people, bring extra instruments, ask others to do the same, and put them in one spot where everyone knows it's ok to use them.

Etiquette in Attending Ceremonies

Contribute Physically

As someone who has put on community events for decades, I am amazed how little some people understand about the tremendous effort that goes into it. There are lots of ways to help out. It makes the leaders FEEL SO GOOD when you do! Yay, support the leaders! Here's a non-exclusive list:

- Read the flyer so you know the details.
- RSVP if you can and come if you said you were coming.
- Bring items that were called for, especially food.
- Offer to give someone a ride.
- Figure out how to get to the location without calling the organizer at the last minute.
- Be on time.
- Ask how you can help. It's a great way to meet people.
- Welcome new people.
- Notice what needs to be done.
- Stick around to clean up if you can.
- If you are already involved, ask for help. Giving people something to do is a gift.

Contribute Energetically

Once the ceremony begins, don't sit back like you're watching a movie. Even if the organizers have made it seem like a show or the ceremony is way low-key, find a way to be connected, even if you have to do it in silence.

- o Give it your full attention. Turn off your cell phone if you are not on-call.
- o Stay off the internet from beginning to end.
- o Keep unnecessary chatter to a minimum.
- o Keep aware of what is going on in the circle if you can. Your awareness strengthens the container.

Privacy

What happens in circle stays in circle. Personal sharing is done with the trust that it will remain confidential. If you really need to talk about something that happened, talk about your own process.

Do not reveal who was there to anyone who is not in the community. People have lost their jobs, their roles in the greater community, and some have even lost custody of their children because of discrimination and fear around anything that does not fit into the big religions.

Don't take pictures unless it is a highly public event or permission is given. This is not just for privacy. It affects the energy of the circle when someone is standing there with a camera. When pictures of the event or the altar are posted online after the fact, that too alters the energy of the ceremony. Ask the organizers first.

Take Care of Yourself

I now, with my sword of personhood that is not any better than your sword of personhood, tap your left shoulder and then your right. I, from now on and forthwith into time immemorial, give you absolute and full permission to leave a ceremony if you are not comfortable with it!

I give you permission to participate in some parts of any ceremony but not in others. I give you permission to close your energetic field and look like you are participating even though you are not because it's important to your friends that you are there.

Just because someone offers a public ceremony doesn't mean that it is a safe environment for you.

You are a sovereign being, and you get to decide what is in your comfort zone and what aligns with your sense of values.

I've guarded myself through a ceremony that appeared to be an attempt to bind members into the community. I've watched ceremonies where grounding was more of a formality than a practice.

I've been in guided meditations where I was being led somewhere that didn't work for me. I went to a ceremony once that looked like a super-cool, magical bling, performance competition. Everyone was wowed by the drama. Lots of people were high. I wanted to throw up. This is all about humans trying to find their way through human foibles into the sacred. Sometimes, we can tolerate it. Sometimes, we can make it work for us. Sometimes, we need to refrain from contributing our personal energy, even with our presence.

If you don't feel good about the intention of a ceremony, you can draw a mental circle around yourself and not participate energetically. You can even take a step back. Yes, politeness is helpful in smoothing the social dynamic, but there is no rule that says you have to open your field. Any social pressure to do so is not ethical magic.

Once I was attending a beautiful ceremony with hundreds of people when someone on stilts suddenly inserted themselves into the center of the circle in order to gain attention or perhaps draw energy from the group. In one moment, my experience changed from the height of excitement to extreme disappointment. Other people didn't seem to mind, but visually, with the differences in height and the person on stilts in the center, the ceremony was no longer about kinship to me. Too upset to continue, I had to walk away.

If the leaders forget to ground, ground yourself. If it seems like a laid-back group, make a call for grounding and they will be grateful for the reminder. If you need space after a ceremony because the power is still moving through you, take it.

Sometimes what people are putting on isn't a ceremony at all. It's just a party. Acknowledge that. Don't try to make it more than it is—and move forward with whatever it is you want to do. If you find yourself in a community that has a different idea of boundaries than you do, and they cannot seem to respect your space, exposing you to unwanted physical affection or intense eye contact, or imposing spiritual interpretations on your experience, get out. Go home. Be true to you.

I have been in ceremonies when I realize that what is going on is vital for the participants' healing but so far from what I am interested in, I need to remove myself so they can have a potent ceremony. I don't want to be a spectator, and I don't want to be sending vibes of annoyance into their container. I would stay if I was invested in supporting their process, but if I showed up with expectations of doing something different, I might be feeling too disappointed to have supportive energy. What is best for me is, in turn, best for everyone, because the more people that align with the ceremony, the more integrity it will have.

Substance-Free Ceremony: Clearlight

If we want a circle to be welcoming to all who are drawn to it, we can't allow mind-altering substances in the ceremony. Period. This is not only a way to keep everyone's focus on the intention, but it is a safety issue, emotional as well as spiritual.

Many, many of us have suffered the consequences of drug abuse in our families, with our loved ones and with ourselves. Many of us are in recovery, on the road to recovery and/or still processing incredibly difficult emotional issues and trauma around these scenarios. If altering substances are present in the ceremony, it will either create ceremony-inhibiting stress, tempt someone to fall off the wagon or estrange people from our offerings.

By themselves, the rhythm of the drum, the dance, the song and the sharing raise our energy and create profound trance states. When we pour out our strong intention and prayers, our sacred space is filled with what I call Clearlight. It shimmers and glows as we become more and more aware of every movement that happens in our circle.

I have seen unbelievable repercussions from the power of invocation. Rippling shock waves. Life-changing energetic shifts. It is a special medicine that cannot be invoked any other way. It is through grounding that the mystery of expansion comes. We may get really far out there, but it is only because we have come from an initiatory space of groundedness.

If someone has a transformative, healing experience and releases unhealthy energies that they no longer need, we want these energies to be grounded, as well as transformed, by the healing energy in the circle and our connection to the spirits of kindness. If someone present is in an altered state induced by substances, they are not necessarily in control of whether their field is open or closed. Without significant training and/or elder support, they may be more at risk of accepting harmful energies into their body. They are also more likely to drift off into an isolated space, no longer in sync with the flow of the ceremony. They might be somewhere interesting, doing something important to them, but they are no longer connected to our collective song.

It even makes sense to stay clear for the whole night, after the circle is closed and into the next day, because there is a delicious cellular story that unfolds after a deep ritual and continues to trace its way throughout our bodies. This delicate time can last a day or two, or a week or longer, depending upon the magnitude of the healing. It is a crucial period to practice self-care, journal, keep clear and find ground. If we don't, our healing process can become convoluted, buried or even reversed.

It is true that there are some ancient traditions that utilize mind-altering substances, though the vast majority of indigenous cultures do not. In these practices, the facilitators have gone through years of training and high levels of initiation in order to keep a very controlled dynamic in the circle. These sorts of ceremonies have become popular in the last decade, but sometimes their facilitators do not have the necessary expertise for all participants to come through safely. Many who enjoy these ceremonies contend that they are good for everyone. They are absolutely not good for everyone. Someone in a crisis may be pushed into more crisis and even psychosis. Some people go into ecstatic states of bliss, yet are never offered the tools to incorporate the lessons they've learned into their everyday lives. Instead, they go seeking the next blissful experience.

These sorts of ceremonies are not necessary. It is not my way. Also, they are intended for personal journeys, whereas the work we are doing here relies on a shared dynamic. In our circle, focused, responsive connection is the heart of the ceremony.

Dream Space

Rest now. It is night.

We have been walking through ceremonial grounds, talking about the ways that we humans bring on change in the intangible realms. After dinner, we will sit under the stars together, and I will tell you of the living spirit of the land which both we and our ceremonies depend on. We will listen to the song of the Mother Bone, which rings throughout the spiral path as all peoples, of stone and stream, of forest and sky, harmonize with her.

The way to truly absorb her song is by feeling its vibration, letting it resound through our bodies and allowing ourselves, like children, to be mesmerized.

Tonight, we will be dreaming awake, together, in the vast dreamscape of her species.

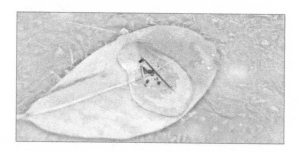

THE MOTHER BONE: ECOSYSTEM

The Mother Bone who feeds us all,
the Mother Bone reminds us.
The Mother Bone who curves the path
and with her song unbinds us.

When we understand how deep the mysteries are, right at the edge of our senses, we grow in wisdom. Eventually, we understand the profound futility of seeking, itself, for seeking gets in the way of listening. We learn instead to live our lives, awake and in constant dialogue with the presence of the interactive, unseen consciousnesses around us. We learn that we can never fully understand these things. It is humbling and inspiring at the same time.

Our personal songs are living microcosms of the greater cycles. The more we pay attention to what is happening around us in the outside world, the more we learn about ourselves and the more of a feast our lives become. When we acknowledge the consciousness of all beings, we discover friends in the fields and allies amongst the winged people. We feel the heartbeat of the great mother who gives life to us all.

We have all heard the song of the straight path, the one designed to lure us to a faraway place where there will be no more pain or suffering. This song is so seductive that even when we know it is telling us lies, even when the curl of the drying autumn leaf tells us otherwise, we still pull away from the spiral cycles of life and death. We know, and we are confused at the same time. As we pull, we leave our own bodies. We make camp in our minds and forget the rest of the world.

We can be so entrenched in our minds that we become folded away in a small back room, stuck behind rooms upon rooms, leading to still yet more rooms, having lost our way to the stairwell, which leads down to the front door and out into the forest. We forget that we *are* nature, our every cell holding the history of another form at another time. We forget, and then we think we are gods, more important than any other creature on the planet, purchasing our goods, devouring them, forgetting that they too are made from the earth we live upon.

Well, she never forgets about us. She whispers in the winds to us when we are sleeping. She blocks the road with big trees on our way home from church. She erodes our creations and heats our tea kettles whether we say thank you or not.

She is a living being that breathes and erupts, washes down the mountains, pours rains upon us and whistles through the trees, spreading seeds of life to take root on fertile ground. She is the great ear, a witness to all that we do. She is filled with intricate, delicate ecosystems, so complicated, we will never understand them.

If you are in search of great treasure,
walk out into the snow.

Visit the forest,
cast out to sea.

Hold your body against the winds,
lie down in the plains,
step into the river.

Look with keen eyes and treasure will surround,
glinting response to your aching.

Bring your burning mind
like a torch into the dark night
with its maze of stars,
and let yourself find silence.

Open to the patterns.
They will dance under your skin,
they will clean out your insides
and later
they will follow you to the grocery store,
to work and back home
until their meaning spills
over the rim,
messy and truthful
relief.

The mother is calling us.

She is not in honeyed images from the tailor,

she is in the heart of the problem

you face on the cliff.

She is in the sound

that steadies.

The mother does not hoard her wisdom.

She opens her hand.

She moves the mountains inside you.

Elemental Forces

Yes, she is all things. She can strike down lightning, splitting a tree in a moment. With a delicate breath, she lifts single leaves, twirling them on their tips. She leaves a billion snowflakes on our doorstep and then melts icicles to feed her spring flowers. She is wild. She never sleeps. She holds space for night stories. She listens to our lives, and she gossips.

The vital energies of her living body are called the sacred elements. They are water, air, earth, fire and universal spirit. In some regions, they are defined differently, adding or substituting metal, wood, void or ether. All have aspects that are sweet and life-feeding when they are in balance. But too much or too little of any one element will bring unforgiving, sure death. It is useful to study their core essences, individually, even though in reality they act in tandem, blending, supporting and even destroying each other. Their energies fuel the spiral continuation of life.

The sacred elements have been called into our ceremonies for millions of years. We draw on their power to make our songs strong. We channel them into transformative prayers. We allow them to wash over us in meditation, as we listen for the messages we need.

However, the further we stray from the sacred spiral, the less we know about them. We think fire comes from a lighter, water comes out of a tap, air is just there, and earth, well, earth is either mucking up the kitchen or somewhere below the asphalt. Numb and disconnected, we wield the raw powers of the earth for selfish purposes. We destroy vast areas of landscape, entire populations. In order to change course, we must recognize and hold dear our connection to Mother Earth, our body being her body, our condition being dependent upon hers. We must own the effects that ripple from our actions.

Many of us yearn for the nature we knew in our childhood. Many of us, raised in cities with cell phones and social media, never had it and are perhaps afraid of it. Even those of us who live close to nature, where it is a constant rather than an event, can forget to live in relationship with it.

Some of us are forced to do our ceremonies in noisy, urban apartments surrounded by power lines, in places where there are so many street lights we never get to see the stars. We might have battery-operated plastic candles, a bowl of water and an over-saturated picture of the mountains over our altar to invoke a sense of the beauty that we know exists. Our ceremony will surely create change, if only through sheer will and intention, but to experience the rich wonder of nature's revelations, in ceremony and out of it, we must reach beyond these symbols to the real thing.

The sacred elements can only be understood through authentic, total immersion in the natural world. We cannot learn about them from a book or a photo or a film. We need to have a rich history of personal time spent out in nature, in the company of our mother, she who is the greatest teacher and who sings the gorgeous overtones of the greater song—the song of the sacred spiral.

When I was young, I was told by Spirit to take the elements on as teachers, each for a year and a day, until I had lived with them all. The first year was Earth, the second, Water, then Air, and then there were two years of Fire which coincided with my entry into political activism.

One secret I discovered is that it doesn't matter how seasoned you are in the ways of the natural world, or how rich your relationship has been with the spirits of the wood, the wind, the water, the fire. It is perfectly possible to spend days in a savage, remote environment, immersing yourself in raw forces of beauty, wondering why you do not feel connected, and then realize you have forgotten to say hello.

But what can I tell you? The truth is, despite all that time being schooled directly by the elements, I couldn't tell you much of what I learned. This is because when nature speaks to us, it is so intimate, so moving, so alive, its fullness can only be grasped in moments of inspiration, within the context of our personal lives. Spiritual potency, like the sacred spiral, ebbs and flows. What once was, has passed, and what will be is unknowable. Our understanding of the elements is ever-shifting as we grow, like a multi-faceted crystal that shows a different view from every angle. Because of this, I can only offer you the Mother Bone songs that are coming through me today. To find her wisdom, you must enter these mysteries yourself.

I long to live in relationship with the land,

speak her language,

sense her shifts, and know my place.

Water

Stepping out of the mire of modern life, I finally reach the shores of the Salish Sea and feel a shift resound across the water. Or maybe it is the landscape inside me. Maybe it is both, I do not know, but it doesn't matter. Water has struck psyche, and my stress releases. This passage back to myself might be long or sudden, but I have learned to trust that it is inevitable—the longer the time spent in such places, the more will be unraveled for me, asking to be picked through.

Step into cold surf

feet caressed

water tugging

through sand

to sea

In the house

a hot bath

steaming fragrant

opens senses

to another realm

Sigh

envelop

heal

home

For me, water has always brought cleansing. It is the contrast of cool on my skin and warmth in the air that I love. It is the untraceable sound of the forested, babbling brook, the rush of falling onto rocks, the danger underneath the soothing.

I love to sit in glacial-carved bowls of rock, under the waterfalls and drench myself. I will always be the kid who loves to spend a whole day swimming, my skin tingling under the hot sun each time I emerge.

My silly water crown,

a star of sprays

Rushing,

breaks over

cold shoulders.

Pounds.

Ka-kaaa!

Here!

Here!

Delicious,

my concave

rock throne.

Fingers of branches
glide downstream.

I am known.
I am loved.
I am kissed in my core
like ice cream.
I am ice cream,
a flavor no one knows

I am a fish.
I have returned to the river.

Today, as I look across the ocean, instead of a blank expanse, I see
a merging of two worlds, sea kingdom and earthly mansion. I know
that my older brother, who loves underwater creatures as madly
as I worship the Redwoods, could write you novellas on its beauty
and feed you secrets he has gathered from his voyages beneath
its surface. I am sure that when he gazes across the flatness, he is
remembering what he has seen underneath and imagining what he
knows might be there.

For me, I like to sit on the black rocks of the Oregon coast and
breathe, as the water crashes against them, watching as icy fingers
flow over broken edges and back into the sea. Something about it
sings to my nature, invokes my wildness and lifts me into prayer. I am
chanting in the wind.

But who cannot be touched when the sun kisses the ocean's lips?
At first, this great water disc, whose expanse fills my vision, shining
mid-twilight, tells me nothing. She is mystery embodied, like a grandmother in grey, full in the face, not silent but still unknowable. She
pulls close her cowl. Even those who know the below and can name
her citizens cannot tell what swells on the other side of the endless
curves that form and reform in the moving realms of the sea.

Then at sunset, she shows it all. Every drop of her splendor, she
describes in mercurial, liquid color which cannot be captured or held.
With each new glance, the masterpieces changes. She spills out the
gold we have been looking for our entire lives, making us feel whole
and glowing with the love we always knew should be there for us.

Then, all color fades from the clouds and the landscape is hollow. With
another swell, the sea becomes a violet faerie land, and we are off
again, enthralled by this new beauty.

This preciousness, reflected inside us, will never fade, and yet it will
fade, if not by morning, within a few days. Such is the way that wisdom
peeks out from the abyss of mystery. We do not understand, and then
we do—for a fleeting moment.

Water cannot be held in the hand. It cannot be shaped or made to stand
up. It knows one thing, which is to flow. Water finds its way into the

smallest crevices with incredible speed. With time, it wears through the most immovable of masses. Oh, time! There is always time! Everything changes with time. Water, wind and heat will always make sure of it.

You cannot break water, but water can be poisoned, and poison us in turn. In water, you can be cleansed and brought back to life, or swept away to your death. But if your body lies in a bog where the water does not flow, there you will lie, awaiting the day when you can be returned to the soil from which you were created. Even death is hindered by stagnant water.

I return to the crashing surf and can no longer feel my wildness. Exquisite spray of white foam collapses over the razor-sharp, black rocks as if there is nothing to be feared. Well, for the water, there isn't.

An eddy between boulders creates a swirling churn of rippled color that unleashed, opens, opens my tangled mind. Thank you. Thank you.

I sing my song, and this time it comes as a low chant, the more mature sound of a woman who has filled in her emptiness and is no longer desperate. The chant swells, containing the history of many meetings with myself and with the land and sea.

You may read these words and think, "Wonderful!" or "I remember!" or "That's not the way it is for me at all!" You may be thinking of the deafening deluge of a monsoon, or wondering how I could miss the feathery quiet of the falling snow. All of these responses make me happy, for you are being brought deeper into your own relationship with the elements. Open. Remember. Describe your unique experiences, and you will find that you are communicating with a raw flow of wisdom.

There are ocean people, mountain people, people of the plains, people of the tundra. Most of us don't resonate with every kind of place. We have our unique heart homes out in the wilderness, and they mean to us what they mean to no one else.

What is your place?

Where does your body come alive?

What place has witnessed your weeping and your joys?

Is it the waterfalls?

The stones?

The swamplands?

The high grasses?

What has taken away your breath,

invoked your prayers?

Where is your temple,

your resonance in our land?

Where do you long to be?

Where do you belong?

Where?

Air

I am not much of a high mountain person, perhaps because of a long life of physical ailments that prevented me from hiking too strenuously. I did try camping in the Mount Shasta area, a place famous for its spiritual energy, but it didn't do much for me.

One of my favorite things, though, is standing in a gale, my arms out, my clothes whooshing past me, feeling every cell of my body being brushed. I love being pushed a little off my balance, too. I can sing into the wind, and no one can hear me. I can speak my troubles. I can say my prayers, and the wind will take them far away to where they will be heard by helping spirits. I can feel the wind removing that which does not serve me, with gentle ferocity.

Through the branches, the whistling wind whispers. It tells me that the ancestors are waiting for me. It tells me of their songs, or perhaps it is the ancestors themselves that I hear through the hollow of the rocks.

I put down my camera and dance with them. I feel the emotions they are moving, in the stomping of their feet. I call for my descendants, this lineage, this backbone of integrity, of seekers holding the line, reminding us that we belong.

I am a flute player. When I play, I am the flute, and the song within me feels like a story. I describe the surrounding scene with my notes as a painter does with stroke and color. In these moments, we are one: myself, the air, the flute. It is my unspoken treatise on the world, my way of saying everything I want to say without having to say it to you. Or anyone. And what is heard by the listener, I have found, may not have anything to do with what I am saying, but everything to do with what they are needing to hear. This is the same way the earth communicates with us. It is a gift to merge with her, even for a passing moment.

I waited inside the charred hollow of a live Redwood

playing my drone flute

Raven

darkness

wrapped in secret shroud tree-ness

I stepped out onto the path

and a woman was weeping

releasing

spiraling upward

trance

trees

flute

I could not stop playing

she could not stop weeping

tears merged

the trees

dropping their blessings

as we passed each other

two women in sun-splashed browns and greens

with padded footsteps

Messages of every kind are conducted through the air, as well as song and smell. This information can come so fast, ceremonialists have come to associate air with the mind. This is only a tradition, so stay with your own winds for now. What do they teach you?

Earth

When I am in the Redwoods, my heart opens like a many-volumed book, its binding undone, spilled across the table. I watch the pages fly, interleaving with the infinite layers of dense, ancient forest around me. Every step I take reveals a new splendor—a lyrical branch, then a haunting tree cave. A shaft of light, then majestic, brushed moss. Always, I see lessons in the patterns of roots splayed before my tiny self. This is my home of homes. In one wet, weekend of walking, I can be turned inside out and set back down as if I've been meditating a week. I don't have words for this. I find myself weeping when I drive down my old familiar pass after a year away, relieved just to be breathing the familiar air. I have had ceremony on dark moons in the black of night under these colossal beings. I have sung my songs, built my fires, played my flutes, and forded the river to reach my grove when spring thaws swept the footbridge away.

I have been given instructions from the Redwoods. I have been told what to bring home. Have been told when to keep out. In my spirit journeys from Seattle, I always travel there first, to ground home, before venturing anywhere else.

When I stand in the Redwood forests, feeling the mass of trees the size of skyscrapers towering above and smelling the needles carpeting the forest floor, I am covered in the gentleness of care. I am aware of how tiny I am in comparison to these ancient, living giants. I can step into the hollows of the trees, lie down and sleep in their charred darkness, wondering at the fact that the trees are still living even after being struck by lightning and fire. When I lay my body on the earth, the ground absorbs my troubles, and I come closer to myself.

I also feel great power when I am near masses of ancient rock. I climb into a cave on the side of a mountain or into a crevice between two boulders, and the earth encloses me. Her presence and silence deafens. There is peace.

High rocks stand daunting on the beach like ancestors,

their sea-beaten faces daring me to heed their message.

Memories are strong here, stories untold.

Speak into the caves your promises, and you will be remembered.

Ask them for favors, and you will be bound to your own truth for life.

Earth, the element that usually lays still, has a way of showing us what is. I form a question in my mind and scan the ground for a stone. I pick up the one that catches my attention the most and then I receive its shape, color and lines as an answer to my question. When I am finished, I place it back, exactly where it was and say thank you.

The ceremonial element of earth is viewed as that which is tangible, solid. Earth provides us materials for our homes, cups to drink out of and tools to work with. It is the structure of our lives, of our schedules and routines, our vocation, our language and our family system, as well as the cosmology of our spiritual path. There is no life without structure—both support and container. Too much structure, however, blocks the flow of creativity and leaves us with stagnation. Life, and living to the fullest, is inherently a dance of constant change.

Additionally, in a marvelous way, the earth holds our collective history, for every cell in our body is borrowed from a living organism of the past. We all came from the earth, and we will all return to it once again.

Fire

Have you stood at the foot of a live volcano, as molten lava oozed and steamed before you? What did you feel? Maybe you could tell tales of the relentless humidity of dense swamplands. Maybe the arid scorch of desert mesas has etched poetry into your veins.

I have had my frosty feet warmed, along with my heart, by my mother's wood stove, hot chocolate between my hands. I have held vigil at a campfire on the cold beach, feeding it for hours, seeing visions in the embers as they collapsed upon each other.

I have looked into a kiln and seen metal transformed into liquid colors so beautiful, I wanted to touch them. And like some of you, I have lit my ceremonies countless times with candles and felt their living presence.

The hearthstone croons,

Stay.

Warm your body.

Dry your boots.

Here is a place of sustenance.

The hearth fire crackles,

Open.

Show your wounds.

Speak your dreams.
Here is a place of confession.

The hearth roars,
Song!
Your poetry!
Your flutes!
Here is a place of cheer.

The hearth hisses,
Closer.
Open.
Stay.
Embers will fade, while
warmth remains.
Here is a place of cherishing.

We lean in,
transfixed,
towards slow-burning flames.

She sighs a sweet hiss,
and the wine of the fire spirit
runs through our hearts.

We are bonded here,
forever fire kin.

The hearth whispers,

Sleep,

I wrap you in my glow.

Dream of stars.

The hearth whispers, *Sleep.*

Metaphysically, fire is associated with our passion and also our rage, our excitement and fervor. The sun's energy exists in every living thing, the pulse of growth, the sprouting of stalks. Fire also cleanses through complete annihilation. When the insurmountable force of a raging wildfire reaches its height, all we can do is try to contain its path, and then wait for it to burn out in its own time. When it is over, what remains is fertile ground.

Center - Spirit

When we are enveloped by the natural world, we sense a presence, a peace pervading everything. It is a blessing just to rest in its being. This presence resides not only in the land, but in ourselves. When we claim it, know its unique qualities, nourish and temper it, we find personal sovereignty. We are present with ourselves and all those around us, and we become just as stunning as a glistening rock in a summer creek, trailing moss in the sunlight.

Beneath our uniqueness, in a state of utmost purity, is an indescribable light. This is the collective oneness, the interconnection between all beings. Perhaps it is the very soul of the planet.

As we gaze at the living landscape, many of us become aware of a light that resides in every creature. The soulfulness of everything, living or not, has been recognized by ancient cultures all over the world, for millions of years. This also includes the soul of an event or a gathering of people, a particular waterfall with its gushing pool, the boulder we climb to watch the sunrise, or the hill where the neighbor kids toboggan every winter. Each has a personality and spirit of its own. All, we can be in relationship with.

When we open our ceremonies, after honoring the directions, we can call on *the center* by bringing our sacred self into presence, while at the same time honoring the sacredness of others, of our circle and the planet herself. The glow of this light holds us, protects us and brings gentleness to our intentions.

Remember, the elements are never separate. Fire cannot burn without air or something to feast upon. Air carries the clouds of rain and snow. Bodies of water are held in the crevices of earth. Earth contains it all, while spirit resides in every center. There are so many intricacies in how the elements in combination express themselves and mirror our rhythms, that our interactions with them become truly personal. The hot sun on a smooth, wet rock beside the mountain river caresses us. A sudden brisk gust, fluttering summer leaves while we ponder a decision, sends warning. Time stretches, our thoughts expand. We are part of the ongoing, melodic conversation between plants, spirits, animals, birds and the winds and waters, from the high alpine to the depths of the seas.

Kiss the Ground

What a wonderful land! What a blessing to be here!

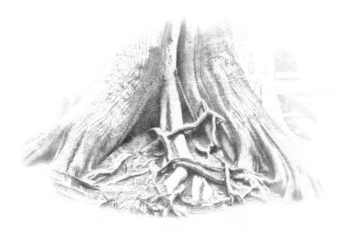

The trees are rustling your name. The canyon calls you to visit her caves. The crisp air and the falling snowflakes descend in swirls of wonder. The streams babble in your ear. Do you hear them?

Follow them. Have your adventure. Steep yourself. When you set out, bring a question. Carry it into the wild and listen with every sense, every fiber of your being. Go as if you are going home, to the origin place of your blood kin. For you are. You are. You are a jewel in the world just as the coyotes' pups are to their parents.

But just one thing, return before dark, for this is our final night. We will feast and afterwards, as we enjoy the fire, I will play my flutes for you.

ʘ

The Spiral Returns

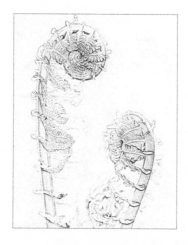

My friend. We are at the end of our journey and the end of our ceremony. The spiral path will soon lead us on, to another place of beginning.

Come. Follow me to this opening in the trees.

I take these ancient bones of ceremony and I give them to you, for they were yours all along. Take them, with all that you've learned, all that you've pondered and all that was useful to you. Call these things into yourself, fuse them with the center of your being.

May your bones sing as your passion blends with the fire of Mother Earth, may your blood flow with the rivers of her body, may your breath join with the winds of the sky, and may your life be a blessing to all of us.

I set down my pack and give you a warm embrace before I head out to my home. I kiss you on the forehead. I bless you.

I hope you know now, about your bones and the specialness of time and space carved with heartfelt purpose. Such sacred events become actual places inside us, places that hold transformative power for years to come.

Share these practices with your people, whether it is your family, a few close friends or a whole pile of them. Help them remember. Enjoy, make mistakes. Laugh about them.

Whenever you are lost, remember that the answer to the question that you've been asking is love. Love will get you to where you need to go. Love is what takes care of you when you think you are alone. Love waits in the corners for you to listen to its voice.

We try so hard to get it right, to learn all these fancy techniques, but the only thing that ever worked and ever will work is love. Love is mysterious, defying definition. That which blocks us from love can be loved. That which holds us back from moving forward can be loved. The only thing that we can reliably put all of our faith into... is love.

If we don't include ourselves in that picture, if we don't strive for self-love, protect ourselves from elements that are not love, broaden our ability to receive love, then there will be vast volumes missing from our understanding. There is always more to learn about love.

I have prepared some gifts for you, to be enjoyed when the time is right. See these bundles here—I place them at your feet. Perhaps we will journey together again, but until then I give you my blessings.

Blessings and Devocation

We thank the Spirits of Kindness
for holding their arms around us
as we journeyed through these teachings.

We thank our named and unnamed spirit friends,
whose benevolence reaches into our lives and
touches us in ways we cannot fathom.

We thank the winds, the high rock, the plains,
the forest, the oceans and all the precious places
we hold dear on this beautiful planet.

We thank the Great Blue Whale,
for inspiring our dreaming and allowing us
access to ancient knowledge.

We return the energies we have invoked to the earth
with trust that the power will come
again when the time is right.

We open our circle and stand in our beauty,
grateful to hear it answered.

May your ceremonies be blessed.

May your ceremonies be filled with love and intention,
and deepen all that you do.

May they lead you through the darkest of times.
May they mirror to the world the way you tend
to your own heart and to those around you.

May your wisdom be remembered.

Merry meet, merry part and merry meet again
Circles within circles and circles again.
Every sacrifice that's ever been made,
every grief, every birth,
every gift that's ever been given and received,
may they weave into our greater tapestry.

May our song be strong.

Blessed Be.

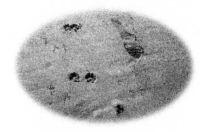

Part III

Gift Bundles for the Road

Bundle of Songs

As you unwrap this bundle, notice its stitching, sewed in bright colors. See the multitude of embroidered pockets. They are brimming with sea shells, some large, some small, and some of the pockets are empty, waiting to be filled. Draw out a shell, my friend. Hold it to your ear, and you will hear the sweet song of a single, cherished ceremony.

Curled in these shells are the old songs. They have been sung, generation after generation, by our ancestors. Their melodies were born in response to the archetypal changes we all experience as we travel the spiral path: changes that surprise us, changes that challenge us and stretch our understanding as to why we are here. Back then, people would feel a change happening and then search for a song, to shape into ceremony.

Songs come when our hearts are connected to the landscape. They are found echoing through sandstone crevices. They slip out between the moon's reflection and the surface of the water. They pour from our tears when our dead are still fresh in the ground. Some are heard in the barking of foxes. This bundle does not hold all the songs of ceremony, for the earth always gives more, each time we ask. Songs come to us when we are in need, when we open our hearts and ask. They come as pure inspiration, with no recipe and no instruction.

As you explore this bundle, you may hear songs that resonate within you while others seem strange. Spend time with the ones you like and the others will sleep until needed. Create your own ceremonies from these songs. Enact them in earnest. Weave their melodies into your life, adding the notes you need. And when you find new songs, borne from your own unique story, place them in the empty pockets. Write them in your journal. Keep them for your descendants.

Rites of Passage

Is there ever truly a beginning or end without the other? Sometimes, it feels that way. Sometimes, all we are feeling is beginning; sometimes the resounding note is of ending and death. And then sometimes, we are in the middle and can't move cleanly forward without acknowledging and honoring both.

Beginnings

My life has become a clean slate. I want to draw on it my dreams of the future, before I unconsciously fill it with things I do not intend.

It is an exciting time when the past is behind us, and the future feels open and fresh. It is a rare opportunity to envision a new life and ceremonially bring it forth. Sometimes, we are so eager to be done with the past, we forget to do this important work, or the new thing in our lives is so big, it is already pulling us ahead. To honor our transition, we need to hold steady and step with awareness. We will find clarity about where we are headed and learn about ourselves as we pay attention to our fears.

Sometimes, a change comes along that we didn't ask for and we definitely don't want. But there's no going back. It is true, we may need to grieve, but at some point, we have to put both feet on the ground and dream the next chapter.

We want to be creators in our world. We want to write our own story, so as each storm of life recedes, we take back the wheel, and we steer. Then we've *really* got something to tell a story about. When you think of it, there are so many beginnings worth celebrating.

What is new for you?

- New school
- New home
- New blended family
- Pregnancy
- New baby, adoption
- New job
- Ground-breaking ceremony
- Releasing your finished artwork into the world
- Engagement
- Wedding
- Blessings upon and commitment to a new path

Portals – Initiation

I've worked hard to gain new life skills. My habits of the past do not reflect who I am anymore. I am committed to going further with these changes and want to enter a new playing field.

Initiations don't come until we've passed through fires of trial and difficulty. A door appears, and we feel drawn to it. We can sense what is on the other side, but we cannot see it. We do know, however, that once we cross, there will be no going back.

This is a sign that we are ready to face and experience the witnessing that usually occurs in an initiation ceremony. Or maybe it is a time to spend a day alone, going through old papers, putting aside the ones we want to burn.

Initiations are threshold-crossings. They can have an element of sorting to them, as we name our accomplishments, identify what we are letting go of, and praise the new things that are showing up in our lives. We can also call out to the goodness we cannot yet see. It's an opportunity to make proclamations and commitments, or perhaps to make a collage that illustrates our intentions.

If you are a parent creating a rite of passage for your children, you are making a tremendous contribution to the larger culture. We need more confident girls in the world. We need more emotionally confident boys, too. We want all our children to feel safe expressing their uniqueness, and we can encourage and reward them for courageous, honorable behavior with ceremony. I will be so excited to hear of the creative ways you come up with to honor your children. Please, share them!

What portals are showing up for you?

- Celebrating the beautiful time of a girl's first menstrual blood
- Boy's coming of age, perhaps when his voice drops
- Adolescent to adult
- First time making love! Some may be lucky enough to know it is coming and want to plan for it
- Young adult leaving home for the first time

- ○ Graduation of any kind
- ○ Change of career
- ○ Stepping into leadership
- ○ Beginning a vocation
- ○ Stepping into activism or service
- ○ Moving across country
- ○ Milestones in sobriety of any kind
- ○ End of grieving
- ○ Realization of middle age
- ○ New self-identification after the death of a parent
- ○ Woman's end of menses
- ○ Adult to elder
- ○ Retirement

Endings

My life has reached the end of an era. I feel as if an unseen gate has permanently closed. I do sense fresh winds of change, but mostly I feel loss and grief.

Sometimes, we need ceremony to finalize drawn-out closure. Sometimes, we need one to let go of someone or something from the past. Ceremony can also create stations of contemplation along a seemingly endless pilgrimage of loss.

Big grief comes with no warning, like a flash flood. We are swept into the river, as dislodged emotions whirl around us. These emotions can be partially revealed, causing confusion, or be compacted in darkness, but at least they are moving now. At least we can feel them. Things will sort themselves out if we can bear to stay present. We cannot stand in a raging river, and we cannot make the waters recede any faster, but someday, our feet will find the riverbed once more.

The emotional complexity of this kind of loss is so huge, it can feel like an overwhelming, tangled mess. So, to survive it, we create periodic moments of clarity. Instead of trying to close the last chapter of life and leave everything behind, we focus on the smaller things we are ready to release. Keepsakes, legal documents, journals, attitudes—we find the things that were once important to us, but now have become burdens. We use ceremony to make a really big deal out of letting them go, and we can't go back. Then, in a few months, we'll be ready to let go of more.

Other endings we are ready for. We experience their finality, and we find that we've already processed our feelings. The wheel of change is turning quickly now, new situations already presenting themselves. Instead of a big releasing ceremony, we can have a smaller one to check in. Is there anything that needs to be said or acknowledged before moving on? Are there new life skills emerging that can be strengthened with praise? Do we want to sing a song or leave behind a token to honor the past?

Here are some common endings that people encounter. What are your untended endings or losses?

- End of relationship, with a partner, friend or spiritual teacher
- Cutting ties with a community that encourages destructive habits
- Ending a course of therapy
- Miscarriage
- Wakes and funerals
- Spreading of ashes
- Leaving the town you grew up in
- Creating a positively formal ending to something that you have been unsuccessful in walking away from
- End of a career or vocation
- Closing a business
- Empty nest (children leaving home)
- Preparing for death

As you explored the rites of passage, did you come across any ceremonies you wished that you had, long ago? The good news is that they can be still be performed in hindsight. This is a powerful form of self-care. They can be enacted alone or amongst a group of friends. They help us release emotional energy we've stored in our bodies from the past.

For example, most of us never had a Coming of Age ceremony.

I never felt like a woman. I was shamed when I had my first menses, and I didn't talked about it afterwards, even with my girlfriends. I want to remove this shame and feel excited about the miracle of my body.

We can pick up the threads of our personal history and gift ourselves with a ceremony designed especially for the part of us that is still waiting to be brought through an initiatory portal. It is never too late to create a rite of passage.

Seasonal Rites

Summer has faded, and I am still riding on the memories of warmer weather. Red and orange leaves of beauty drop before me, and I barely notice. I want to feel inspired and present with the season as it turns.

It's easy to lose track of the seasons when we spend so much time indoors. Instead of being open to the wild, variant beauty of every moment, we complain. We push and we pull, and we miss the invitation to participate.

Cultures around the planet throughout history have aligned their practices with the turning seasons. We can do this too, by feeling the seasonal energy in the air and calling it into our ceremonies. At any time of year, both gifts and lessons are available. They exist in the tendrils of new life, the burst of growth, the full bloom. They are in the harvest and the letting go. They are in the withering, the final death and the great dreaming of the next curve along the spiral path.

Here in the Pacific Northwest, when the sun finally peeks through the clouds after months of haze, it does so for a few moments at a time. People literally drop what they are doing and rush outside to garden, or just to stand in the street with their faces upturned, feeling life rush back into their skin. Later, when Spring actually does come, the energy is intoxicating. Luscious greens sprout hope, even as gentle rains continue.

Mid-Summer, the clouds roll away, revealing the mountains. We pull weeds from our gardens and play outdoors late into the night. When Autumn comes, the angle of the sun paints everything in twilight golds. Then we rest, at the edge of things. In appreciation and reflection, we harvest our fruits, and then we let go. The days get shorter, and we move indoors with our tea and books for another long season of winter nesting.

Even though our weather is mild and snowfall is rare, winters here still carry the sacred deathly energies. We hibernate in the dark. We digest and dream over the past. Mid-Winter, feeling lost in the long night, we sense a shift, and the days start to grow longer. From then on, we dream in the new. Our dreams form slowly, and when the ground warms, we plant them as seeds into the beds of our lives. We wait, sprouts come, and the year turns once again.

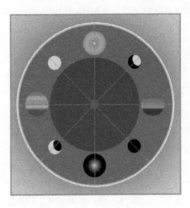

What is it like in your hometown? How do you mark the seasons? What signals their change to you? If you aren't sure, there is something you can do to become more attuned. Commit to eight seasonal celebrations over the span of one year, and a new body of knowledge will open itself to you.

Four of these days are the Solstices and Equinoxes. Solstices are the darkest and lightest days of the year. You can think of them as the nadir and peak of creative energy, a good time for visioning or manifestation, respectively. Equinoxes are the opposite quarters, between the

Solstices. These occur when the pull towards darker days and the pull towards brighter days are perfectly balanced. These rare moments of stillness allow for a broader perspective, free from seasonal forces. There are also cross-quarter holidays that happen right between the Solstices and Equinoxes. Instead of thinking of them as the in-between markers, hone in, and notice their unique seasonal nature.

All eight of these days together are called *Sabbats* by the pagan Northern European traditions. It's fun to research, and easy to find details about the traditions practiced on these holidays, but if you haven't lived in the places that are being written about, I would suggest you design your own ceremonies. For most of us, stories of historical rites describe seasons of faraway lands in long ago times, performed within the context of cultures we cannot fully understand. Instead, live, breathe and be present with what is around you.

You can celebrate simply for seasonal attunement, but you can also use the seasonal energies to infuse any of your ceremonies, for example, by having a releasing ceremony in the late fall. If the season does not match your intention, instead of aligning to the Wheel of the Year, tune into the cycle of a day. One full day, from sunrise to the next sunrise, is a microcosmic expression of the annual life/death cycle. So, you would call to the West as the sun sets, in the place of letting go.

Private Ceremonies for Our Loved Ones

Someday, you may feel called to gift a loved one with a personal ceremony. They may be coming out. A close friend may have seen their house burn down. Perhaps your child is showing signs of entering that wild ride of adolescence. I cannot express how powerful this sort of gift is. All that love, time and energy will create a lasting impression. The ceremony will validate their experience, and if they are in hard times, ease their suffering.

I always ask permission of the person, and I never plan the entire thing. I sit with them and ask them what they need to get out of it. When I listen to how they feel, I get clues as to what might work for the ceremony. Together, we figure out what symbolism would be resonant for them, and which elements they cannot live without. I make sure we are on the same page with the intention. Then I tell them that there will be something special planned they won't know about. Because we have had this meeting, trust is built, and I am able to safely get creative. I ask my helping spirits for insight.

You can't do this ceremony without knowing the other person's heart. Imagine planning a coming-of-age ceremony for a young man who thinks becoming an adult means taking on a leadership role, when you think it means learning to express his emotions responsibly. Or imagine planning a grieving ceremony without knowing where the recipient is in their grieving process. It could be a disaster, hurtful even, because your loved one doesn't feel heard.

I ask the recipient who to invite, and then I make sure the people who are invited are going to be one hundred percent on board and not uncomfortable with ceremony. We must have a safe container. I tell the recipient they are not allowed to do any planning. They get the wonderful task of allowing others to give. They can't even bring a cookie. Maybe a friend will even give them a ride!

Some people like gifts. Some people appreciate time. Some are touched most deeply by words. Others are moved by the effort you contributed. Fulfill all of these things, and they will feel loved.

After the ceremony, be sensitive to the fact that the recipient might need time to process and not be ready to socialize. Maybe you can build private time into the post-ceremony, offering a respite room while everyone else gets the celebration part going. Maybe the ceremony is the main event, and then everyone goes home.

In our highly individualistic, competitive culture, the privileged are too often held high while everyone else is left to their own devices. It is a precious thing to hold ceremony for someone else. If you are called to this, thank you so much for focusing your care towards someone who really needs it.

Emotional and Physical Healing

I have been struggling for so long, I don't know what it feels like to be healthy. I have help from medical practitioners and a counselor, but something is missing. I need to work on my recovery in a spiritual way as well.

Many of us know we need ceremony for healing. Often, we want it to happen all at once, like a miracle. Some of us have been through so much trauma, we don't believe that healing can ever be finished. It is true that miracles happen, but more often than not, healing is a long, cyclical process. Some of us were given a bunch of hardship at the beginning of life while others seem to get their hardship parsed out more slowly. What is for sure is that there is no life free from injury. Please know that it is possible to find peace and balance. We can nourish our inner strength, and we can clean up our lives. It just takes time.

Healing ceremonies can resolve immediate confusion and soothe the pain of the present. This relief may last a day, a week or several months, but one ceremony by itself is usually not the solution. After our ceremony, we must incorporate the lessons we learned and keep moving through the layers of healing, towards the source of love that resides in our hearts. Sometimes, we feel we are completely healed, even for a year or so. Then, more pain surfaces, pain that could not come through when we were unstable and feeling unsafe. So, we return to ceremony.

Every time we undergo healing, our core becomes more solid. We become stronger and the process of healing becomes more familiar. The times of peace that come between cycles of chaos and growth extend. Feeling safer allows our awareness to broaden. As we learn to recognize our unique needs around when to establish boundaries and when to be vulnerable, we become resistant to troubles that tripped us up in the past. We are able to be more present in the world. Energy previously misspent rushes through us, asking us to go even further, to create what we were always called to, with more purity this time.

Many of us carry a primal wound that affects every aspect of our lives. It is, curiously, often connected in some way to our primal gifts. This wound is so deep and sensitive, we cannot mend it until we have paid much attention to other wounds. Once we do, our primal gifts are able to blossom.

Ceremonies to Support our Personal Sovereignty

I don't know where I start and other people begin. I feel like everyone has a piece of me. I don't know who I am anymore.

There is a spiritual law of sovereignty that states that no one should enter our energetic field or personal space or touch our body without our permission. Our body and energetic field together make up our most sacred temple for the time we are alive on this planet. This is our sovereign domain, and it is our privilege and right to protect it.

Unfortunately, it isn't unusual to find ourselves carrying around energies of the past or holding the emotions of other people. Our thoughts can also become entangled with the voices of unhealthy cultural ideology, transmitted by the media and our social networks. Often, we don't even realize how much we're weighed down until the excess energy is released, and we come back to ourselves. Through ceremonies of clearing and protection, we support the health of our bodies and energetic fields. Here are some intentions and ways to clear our fields, fill up with nourishing energy, or expand ourselves through exploration:

- Divest energy from activities/media/relationships that are unhealthy for us and call that energy back into our body.
- Reflect on whether we energetically hold onto other people, and consciously return their energy.
- Call ourselves back into presence with ourselves.
- Find inconsistencies in ourselves, and restore integrity/alignment with ourselves.
- Account for and express gratitude for our personal gifts.
- Call back life's passions, once forgotten and now missed.
- Spend a silent day as a student of nature.

Once we feel clear, it will be easier to stay clear if we establish for ourselves certain habits. What helps you feel clear? Do you need to incorporate physical movement into a brief, daily ceremony? Do you need to sing more? What would support your sovereignty in an ongoing way?

Here are some structures we can put in place.

- Establish an area in our home as a place for spiritual practice. Set up and bless our altar.
- Create a private, sacred space around our creative activities so we can expand our expressive language.

Too many of us have suffered trauma from abuse, be it verbal, physical, sexual. We are made to feel ashamed of our gender, sexual preference, race, heritage or body shape. We are thrown out of ourselves, disconnected from our bodies. This is serious. We can reach for help from therapists and healers, but we can also perform ceremony to reclaim ownership of our own body and our sense of self. Here is a ceremony skeleton for you to fill in with your personal bridge of symbols.

1. Have a sensuous bath with scented salts and candles, then cover yourself with a favorite lotion or oil. Honor and celebrate each part of your body.
2. Dress in your favorite comfortable clothes. Then, go into sacred space and meditate on what personal sovereignty means to you. Do some writing and list the things about

yourself that you love, even if they include activities you haven't done in a very long time. Write down your core values.

3. Establish personal, physical and psychic boundaries, using a wand or a pretty stick from the woods to draw a line around your body in sacred space. You can even use charcoal to mark your body with symbols, signifying your beauty and your steadfast values. Perhaps this will become a new design for a tattoo?

How can you turn this into a ceremony that words for you? What do you need to feel at home in your body? In your sense of being? In your world? What do you need to say? Do you have something to shout?

Unmuddying the Waters

The difficulties just keep coming. There is too much to process. I don't know who or what to trust. I can't remember the last time I felt joy.

Overwhelming hardships are difficult to process. There can be so much out of our control, we can no longer see clearly. On top of this, emotions from the past can be triggered, creating more confusion.

Sometimes, we need a ceremony simply to find clarity. We can still our minds through a quiet practice such as meditation or divination. We can also explore our thoughts, feelings and needs by speaking aloud, dancing or engaging in other forms of creative expression. As we express and release, we gain greater perspective on our hardships as well as our relationship to these hardships. We find ourselves able to chart a course with a clearer eye.

Here are some ways to find clarity through ceremony.

o Express ourselves in sacred space through visual arts, writing or music to get what we are feeling out of our systems, leading to better perspective.

o Dance our emotions long enough to allow them to shift into new feelings.

- o Speak aloud everything we need to say
  until there is nothing left to say.
- o Ask for direction and/or healing from the spirits of kindness.
- o Use divination to explore what the trouble is.
- o Using meditation, identify the everyday signals that
  will let us know when to take a break and reflect so we
  can experience more clarity throughout the day.

Healing for the Land

*Ahh! Mother Earth! What can I do? Your land is pillaged. Our waters
are poisoned and filled with micro-plastics. Your body is dismembered
by blasting in the mountains. Every day, more species become extinct.*

This is a crisis. Many of us feel panic as report after report tells us of
global temperature rise, melting polar caps and what seems to be a
looming, inevitable point of no return. How can we reverse the atroci-
ties that are being committed and bring back the natural balance? Are
we helpless?

Some say we need to spiritually heal the earth. Some say she will take
care of herself, likely by getting rid of us humans. If you are looking for
a ceremony to stop the destruction, there isn't one. The only way we
will end the madness is by defending our home. We must join organiza-
tions that manage environmental protection and restoration projects.
We must advocate for green energy and stricter environmental poli-
cies. We must stop buying products that were unethically produced or
designed for a fast track to the landfill. If we don't do these things, in
a few short generations we may all be dead.

At the same time, we can heal our *relationship* with Mother Earth by
going to the places we cherish on this planet. As we express our love, we
in turn learn to love ourselves. We are of the land. There is no difference
between us. The sooner we learn to love ourselves, the sooner we will
learn as a race to extend respect and love to the one that supports us
all, the greatest Bodhisattva, Mother Earth. And just as we honor our
human loved ones who have passed on, we can honor the species who

have become extinct, offering them our apologies and our love, and prayers for their souls to rest in peace.

When the trees speak, what do they say to you?

Do they say, I miss you?

Do they say, I have been ravaged?

Do they touch your every cell like velvet, caressing your woes?

Do they give you insights when you call from your pain?

The trees are speaking.

They are leaning towards us.

They are dreaming for

someone to listen.

Manifesting

My rent was raised, and I have thirty days to find a new place. I don't want to leave the neighborhood and make my kids change schools. We need a home that has enough room for us all, and allows pets, too!

There are times when we need something practical or tangible to come into our lives. The action of calling something from the ethereal into the physical is called manifestation. Manifesting something specific can be tricky because when we send our intentions, it is very easy to draw something extra to us that we did not intend but we unconsciously desired. This could be advantageous, or it could be a big mistake. To prevent this, we call out for qualities we desire without naming particular places, times or objects. Adding a statement to our intention such as "I am manifesting this or better" allows unexpected blessings to come into our lives.

Remember to avoid directing intentions or energy at other people without their permission. If we are worried about stray thoughts or unconscious emotions, we can add the common disclaimer, "For the good of all, according to free will." Here are some things we typically do for manifestation ceremony.

- o Manifesting a new job
- o Manifesting a new home
- o Drawing to us the qualities of love we desire, without naming or thinking of any specific person
- o Manifesting easy travel logistics, running into the right people, making the right connections, a way to get to that concert!

Devotional Ceremonies

I want to offer my gratitude to the spirits of kindness for all the support and healing they have given me. I also want to know them better, outside of the times when I am asking for help.

It's nice to create a special ceremony just to spend time with the spirits of kindness. It's true, they walk with us every day, setting out signs for us to notice or whispering in our ear, but sometimes we long for a more tangible communion. We long to immerse ourselves in their beautiful presence and healing energies. We want to let them know in a big way how grateful we are for their friendship.

This is how to offer sweet, devotional ceremony. First, choose the spirits of kindness that you want to show devotion for. This could be the angel Ezekiel, or the archetypal spirit of dolphin. It could be Kwan Yin or Cernunnos, or it could be a recurring unnamed presence, such as "the beloved" or "the lady of the deer." Create sacred space in a way that works best for you and invite them to join you. If you are inviting a mythological deity known to carry imperfect human characteristics, such as Odin or Kali, be sure to invite only their compassionate side. Life is difficult enough. We don't need to be inviting more trouble than we already have.

When you are finished with your invitations, the devotions begin. Speak directly to them. Describe how you experience their presence, how you feel about them and how you feel they support you. Listen with your whole body for any response to your ardor, but do not stop. Just keep going. Pour your heart out. Be honest.

Powerful stuff, yes? Imagine expressing this kind of adoration for another person. It would blow their mind. Think of the Shakespearean sonnets of love. Think of the Buddhist mantras, old-time gospel singing, the Hindu practice of kirtan. These forms of devotion consist almost entirely of song, chanting or poetry because of how difficult it is to describe the profundity of grace. The repetition practiced in devotion can bring on an ecstatic state. We are sent deep into trance. Our confidence in our love builds and when the spirits respond, we feel their sweet energy rush in. Bliss bursts like a radiant star. In this moment, we come into union with the divine. Our hearts, mind and body are merged on a vibrational level, and we are changed. This is a love affair.

You can do devotional ceremony any way you want. You can dance, hum, read your own poetry, even love letters to your spirit friends. If you are filled with brimming gratitude already, you can pour that out to the spirits of kindness in glowing, silent appreciation. Before you are finished, you will find yourself caught up with the spirits in mutual celebration.

There are some of us, however, who may react defensively to the suggestion of offering devotion. We have already left an organized religion out of ethical conflict, and our wounded hearts do not want to open again. We are wary of any leap of faith endangering our hard-won sense of personal sovereignty. But secretly, behind the defensiveness, many of us haven't lost our faith. We have lost our trust in organized religion. We still sense—or at least remember—the presence of the divine.

The kind of leap we need in order to be in a devotional state will not breach our sovereignty. All we need to do is choose to be receptive to the goodness we already know is there, constant and trustworthy, holding us dear. We don't have to give anything away or make commitments. We can just chant the name of our beloved spirit. We can be present with its pure essence, and see if it makes us feel better. This subtle shift from being guarded to being open in a safe way can open a door for new perceptions, even a new relationship with the loving spirits. It has the potential to ignite unimaginable change in our lives.

The Spirits have carried me through times of crisis, but now that the drama has passed, I tend to forget about them. I feel guilty about this and want to feel their presence once again.

Just as in any intimate relationship, when we drift from them, we long for them. The magic seems to drain out of the world. Sometimes, we feel that we don't deserve their goodness. But they offer us no blame or shame. The spirits of kindness come from a place of pure, unconditional love. They are waiting, loving, even helping us when we are not aware. It's also impossible to accept too much from them. The awe we feel under a starry sky is infinite star-ness. We drink that beautiful feeling into ourselves, and the stars are not diminished. There will always be more.

There are so many ways we can be blocked from having a relationship with the divine. Some of us feel that God has betrayed us by not removing hardship, but no religion ever promised that spiritual connection would shield us from pain. Life is just so much more manageable when we are in a flow with the divine. Our minds tend to clear more quickly; we have a broader perspective. We are supported as we walk through life, and this allows us to learn from our hardships.

Some of us are waiting to be told what to do, like the voice of God in a Noah's Ark movie, but spirit usually communicates through inspiration, not words.

It's also possible to become spiritually over-confident, leaving the spirits of kindness behind.

My spiritual life has become predictable. I do work with the loving spirits, but too often I find myself deciding what their influence will be in my ceremonies. I am not sure if their participation is in my mind, or if it is really happening. I feel there is something missing.

In devotional ceremony, we restore our connection to mystery, inviting play and the unexpected. There is no hierarchy in relationships with the spirits of kindness. Neither party answers the other's bidding out of obligation. It is true that the spirits of kindness are greater wisdom-keepers and sources of healing than we could ever be, but they need us just the same. They long for us to tap into our own divinity and realize our calling. When they are successful in helping us do that, our presence shines and becomes a gift to those around us, reflecting their own light back. This makes the spirits very happy.

After having explored this bundle of shells, after having listened to many songs and contemplated the ones that resonate with you, please accept one more gift, to help you stay true to your ceremonial intentions.

Flip back through the book to the Bone of Intention.

Sweep the magic wand off the page.

The air sings with its motion, sings, "Integrity."

Its magic was gestating while we journeyed.

Each step you took, each question you answered for yourself made this gift more potent. The more we know ourselves, the more time we spend asking hard questions and honoring our heart's needs, the more in line with natural cycles of creation our ceremonies become. This wand is the tool that holds us to our intended path throughout our ceremony creation and enactment process.

Now, sweep it into your heart.

Know that it will keep your intentions pure,

wrapped in love, so you will do no harm.

This wand will steady your mind

as you build your bridge to the otherworlds.

Direct your intent, and it will not waver.

Blessed Be.

Bundle of Light in the Darkness

Nestled, deep inside us all, is an exquisite light, a source of pure love. When we feel safe, this light blossoms and the whole world is sweeter. And when we are able to see the shine in others, it is so wonderful, or funny, or enticing, we want to tell stories about it.

We need to tell each other stories describing the beauty that we find, the way to beauty and the ways of survival in times that are not beautiful. In fact, it is essential for us to do so because it keeps our hearts open. When there is nothing worth telling stories about, we are no longer seeing, or shining.

Long ago, before the radio or television, storytelling and music were the main sources of entertainment. Especially in the winters, people would gather near a central fire after dinner. While crafting or sewing by candlelight, while playing music or sitting on the laps of elders, they listened to stories to celebrate, to delight, to give hope and to call in dreams. In many cultures, there were designated story-keepers. They held the teaching stories, which kept the cultural cosmology alive. Some were epics that took weeks to tell. Others were healing stories. When the community lived through important times that shifted their viewpoint or traditions, new stories were created.

Many of these stories still exist, convoluted though they may be from multiple translations, and many of them still hold valuable lessons. But there was a break in the line of stories passed down through the generations, when storytelling ceased to be integral to social evolution.

At the same time, there have always been stories to fill us with doubt and cloud our vision. When we listen, our blossoms contract, diminishing our light and others cannot find us. We look up at the greatness of the universe and we feel small, instead of in union with it. These kinds of stories serve to drain light from the listener and give it to the teller. The teller, not the story, becomes the vast universe, while the listener becomes disempowered, vulnerable to suggestion.

The shouter's stories are like this. They are so loud, they drown out our own stories until many of us give up trying to tell them. Then our stories fade.

Predatory stories have spread so far across the planet, few of us are untouched. We dream of endless summers on tropical beaches. We quest for notoriety instead of contribution. We search for that place at the end of the straight path where we will no longer feel pain. We are told that money will get us there, and we want it so badly, we are willing to walk upon the weak through both our earning and our spending. We are constantly inundated with the shouter's songs of the straight path through ads, radio, media and even our loved ones' words. In a quick morning commute, before we are fully awake, our bodies can experience the vibrations of dozens of influences, all asking us to open our wallets or be something we are not. *Buy this. Feel this. Want this. Strive to be something you could never be.* We try to block them out, but when we are not strengthened by our own stories, born from our own songs, we cannot. Our beautiful minds, which drink so deeply and crave stories so strongly, think that any story is better than no story.

So, we must find and tell our stories, for ourselves and for each other. We must share our joys and our hardships. We must frame our stories in a healing perspective. We must sing, for if we don't, the greater song will be lost forever. To do this, each of us must find our light, embody our light, shine in our unique way and show each other who we are. When we weave our stories, filled with the light from our hearts, into the greater tapestry of song, they will continue to teach and inspire, lasting long past our time.

But first, we reclaim our goodness.

Unraveling the Curse of Original Sin

One of the greatest curses cast upon the human race in the last few thousand years is the concept of original sin. Some religions insist it is incurable. Others claim that it can be wiped clean with baptism. Regardless of theological interpretations, many of us who are laypeople carry a deep-seated sense of being an *awful, rotten, bad person*. Shame is the great motivator for many of our actions, often without our realizing it.

This curse struck not only those who believed in original sin, but everyone else too, as it was distributed through the collective psyche. Too often, events, people and situations are qualified as good or bad, which traps them in a fixed state, not allowing them to be multi-dimensional. When we are good, we can look down on the bad, while still afraid of being bad. When we are bad, we can never be good. Either way, we cannot grow.

I cast down this curse. You are not bad. There is no mark on your soul.

Love yourself. Trust that underneath all your layers is a preciousness that has been there since birth. Everyone has had a messy life, done things they regret. Yet, history is full of people who have come back from the blackest of places. Once we realize that, the nature of darkness changes. It becomes a gestating place, a place of replenishment, a place of dreaming, a space of blessed mystery. In truth, darkness holds a brilliant light, a light which cannot exist without darkness. Embrace the complexity and wholeness of yourself. Forgive yourself.

Give yourself the time and nurturing you need. Be open. Be generous, not because you are shamed into it, but because it is a joyful thing to be.

The source of love inside each of us comes packaged in this incredible thing called joy. I went through years of suffering to discover it, and when I did, it was so visceral, so safe, I couldn't turn my back on myself anymore. I restructured my life and chose years of solitude, rather than give into unhealthy situations that would make me lose touch with myself again. I needed silence so I could tap into my own song. I discovered what it meant to love myself. I had no idea what that meant before. So I can tell you, without a doubt, that you can do it, too.

You can physically, metaphorically and spiritually reject the dark mark that power-hungry people, long ago in history, cast upon your soul. Say no and have a ceremonial cleansing. State, describe and dance the brightness that is in you. Loved ones can help you along the way, but no one can truly protect that light, nurture that light or share that light but you. Free yourself. Free us all by showing us the way.

Rejecting the Harmful Stories in the Media

Just as we need to reclaim our goodness, we need to remove the societal influences from our psyches that lead us away from our core values. Much of the messaging that comes from the corporate media serves to amplify the shouter's stories and songs, filling the air around us. It is psychologically unsafe, so we need to be smart. We need to be sharp. Let me tell you a secret...

The reason why stories in the media are so entrancing is that they contain many elements of ceremony. People who design these experiences are systematically trained in how draw us into a trance state via the beauty of seductive images, the shock of violent images or with provocative images of scenarios we might long for. Enclosed in the womb of a movie theater, or nesting with our computers in the apparent safety of our homes, we let down our guard. Then they have us. Vulnerable to suggestion, our psyches are penetrated with desire to consume products. As we become accustomed to the adrenaline rush of violence and fear, we reach out for more. Our vulnerable minds quietly, subconsciously take on the characters in the stories as role models. At each commercial break, we are imprinted with complex logos, containing color, shape, feeling and sound. Any of these traits can trigger a memory of the logo throughout the day, interfering with our thoughts and encouraging us to consume.

We are drawn in because of our loneliness, our need for escape, or simply our natural hunger for storytelling. Then we pay a high cost. We think that we are immune to the crudity and violence, but we have just become numb. Far below the surface, our dreams, our thought patterns and our relationships are still actively being shaped.

This is a serious, insidious misuse of magic, filled with curses, consciously or unconsciously designed to drain us of our personal power. Just as we choose how deeply we want to participate in other people's ceremonies, we must choose which stories we allow to be poured into our consciousness. We also need to check in and ask ourselves what we are getting out of the media we already consume. Sometimes, we are being taught lessons, or presented with situations that mirror our own lives. Sometimes, we favor certain genres or character types that carry archetypal forces, steeped with deep, complex meaning. Perhaps we watch a lot of family shows in order to feel a sense of family. Or we choose to witness documentaries of genocide so we can educate ourselves and hold those people with love. Sometimes, the violence in a show reflects back something happening in our own lives, or maybe we just like the adrenaline.

If the adrenaline rush triggered by a story does not lead to something transformative, educational or healing, it can only lead to addiction. Addiction is what the media makers want. Once we are hooked, their spells flood us with stories which cover over any memory we have of the best story imaginable, the one inside us, the story of our personal song.

If we are to live fully, we must be smart, get clear. If we don't know how to moderate our intake, we must choose silence over cacophony. If fear rises from the thoughts and emotions revealed in the silence, know this: *Some of those feelings are the heart's hunger, calling for ceremony.* We may not be able to get clear before ceremony, but we can create ceremony to get clear and then over time, our song will emerge.

Try a media fast. Instead of avoiding thoughts of media, think deeply about it. Make a list of your favorite shows and prioritize them. Write down how each one hooks you, or how you benefit from it. Notice how time stretches when you have space in your day for other things. Sit with the silence and see what you might find yourself interested in doing. If the silence feels intolerable, ask your heart if it is longing for a life change, or a ceremony.

Try a social media fast. Notice how it feels in your body to be offline. Write down your reasons for being on social media and also what you don't like about it. Create for yourself a social media policy. For instance, disconnect from all sources of information that make you unnecessarily emotional. Perhaps there are people you don't need to be thinking about. Maybe you want to change your privacy settings so that only people you trust see what you post. Maybe you feel deeply about the fact that everything you write, in private or public spaces on social media, is being surveilled by automated databases. What if you promised yourself to call a friend when you feel upset, before deciding to post? Or maybe you could write a long email about the topic and then send it to yourself. Maybe your life would be better completely free of social media. Find out what is truly best for you.

Singing the World Back into Balance: Reclaiming Our Collective Psychic Space

Social norms do not reflect my values or my need for honesty and intimacy. I feel the forces of discrimination pushing in on me, and I am tired of seeing those I care about being marginalized. But who wants to fit into a culture of competitive, consumerist greed? We are all feeling alienated, disconnected, but no one is speaking up or reaching out.

With such great forces working against us, it would be easy to feel despair, but we have more power than we know. We can the sow the seeds of balance and reclaim our collective psychic space through formal ceremony.

In ceremony, we can sing our dreams of a new future. We can dance in the energies to help us heal. We can send clarity to a situation where there is confusion, miscommunication and conflict. We can ceremonially release anger from the atmosphere of a situation by asking for it to be transformed into right action. We can soften the collective fear around speaking to society's illnesses. We work on the energetic plane, before ideas are manifested into form. This is all done without interfering with anyone's free will or sovereignty. By focusing on collective patterns and not individuals, we do not hurt anyone.

It would be senselessly dangerous to get in the middle of destructive energies and try to change them. Instead, we connect to the web of light, the greater song and our spirits of kindness.

We remember our beloved elements and aspects of nature, invoking this power instead of using our personal energy to counter forces too great for any individual. We do all this without ever leaving our sacred space.

We raise the energy, shape it with our intention and with the help of the spirits, send it into a symbol we have prepared to represent the situation we are affecting. The energy passes through, to the other side, to the macrocosm.

Writing Our Own Stories,
Creating Authentic Culture

We can also be intentional about creating organic culture for ourselves. Culture is supposed to be shaped by humans and the energies of the land, not corporations. Profit-driven corporations do not create a culture of kindness or empathy. They are not part of our community. They do not eat, live and die according to the laws of Mother Earth. And yet they dominate the airwaves. In order to reclaim culture, we have to take the public storytelling platform back.

When we become clear of harmful influences of the media, we earn back space in our lives which we can fill with authenticity. We can hear ourselves think again, enabling us to focus on the real issues in our lives.

We sing our song, and in doing so, we remind others of their song. Then, we have people to sing with. The greater song rises and gently embraces us as we walk the spiral path. Our songs, being truly authentic and alive, are mysterious, shifting and changing, like a sunrise. They can never be entirely understood. This is why we tell stories about them. We want to remember the times that changed us. We want to share in the delights and sorrows. We want to honor the struggles and record the teachings, to pass to our descendants. These stories give us something to hold onto, something to lead us back to our own songs when we are lost.

Community ceremony is one expression of our collective song that naturally becomes story. But sadly, it is another arena that has been muddled by unhealthy societal systems. Many people stay in churches that abuse them because they need ceremony and community. Many return to the same churches they left because they want these things for their children. They feel that a compromised ceremony is better than no ceremony at all.

We don't need that anymore. We can take back authorship, song and ceremonial creative rights, too! We can create formal ceremonies to mark our transitions, and we can also build nourishing traditions, weaving them into the tapestry of our lives. What community traditions do you already have that can be given special, ceremonial attention?

Every summer, our family goes to the ocean for vacation. On the first day, we always take a walk together. During this walk, we all look for a stick that calls out to be picked up. Before the week is out, we carve a pattern in our stick that expresses the best part of ourselves. We describe our sticks to each other; then we bring them home to place on the mantle. In times of difficulty, we gather after dinner and take the sticks down, sitting in a circle. We pass our sticks to the left and then each person describes what they remember about them. This strengthens our family, builds personal confidence and reminds us to see the best in each other, instead of fighting. When the year is up, we travel to the ocean again and return our sticks to the sea.

In my group of friends, we like to tell stories about funny things that happened, or dramatic events in our history. Whenever someone passes through a hardship, we celebrate with them, with a new story of their struggle and their bravery, highlighting at the end the gift the person found, and how it is a blessing for us all. Sometimes we gather for storytelling nights. We always have a candle, a bell to begin the evening, and our famous tomato soup.

When we spend a lot of time with the same people, common practices, stories and inside jokes emerge. Pulling a few of them out and turning them into ceremony or tradition is what I would call the beginning of a true, organic, spiritual culture. When we tell stories about the transformative times we shared, we bring to life our heroic sagas.

Carrying Sacred Tools in the Mundane

There are countless wonderful ways we can use our ceremonial tools to bring meaning into our daily lives. It's not the same as enacting a full ceremony because we cannot safely allow ourselves to go into a deep trance outside of sacred space. But we can still make powerful use of the language of ceremony: symbols and song, language and dance.

In fact, there are some changes that cannot be accomplished through full ceremony and yet must be attended to. In this case, we identify the change we need and then amplify our idea using the power of our words and symbols. We design educational campaigns. We create inspiring digital media. We advocate. Private investigators dig up the truth and publish it for the world to see. Then we boycott products, subcultures and media that are not good for us. We divest our energy and money from corporations that fund unethical projects.

We speak in the language of living symbolism by using our artistic talents. The creative potential here is tremendous. We create public artwork. We write music and perform our poetry. We concoct zany, meaningful flash mobs. We support our activist sisters and brothers in their work. I've seen hundreds of people dressed as sea turtles waddling down 5th Avenue in Seattle during the WTO (World Trade Organization) protests, to bring attention to the eroding restrictions on fishing practices that kill sea turtles. I've seen a river of salmon on painted banners, swimming and leaping in glowing light at the demonstrations for the Salish Sea. These living symbols are emotionally evocative, giving demonstrators more energy for their cause. Their playfulness also eases potential tension in the crowd, keeping people safe.

Having learned to connect with the spirits of kindness in ceremony, we can also bring this experience into our daily lives. We open to the nourishing beauty in the pause of someone's expression, the reflection of a stream, in the ribbons of life. Aware that each of us has a sacred song, we can listen for it in the people around us, even when they themselves are not aware they have one. And when we are tired and overwhelmed, we ground ourselves as we have learned to do, before and after our ceremonies. Oh, the wonders we work in the vast eco-system of people who are writing, building, serving, holding space and lovingly creating change in dynamic diversity, where every job, every role is as crucial as the next.

We can use our sacred tools to touch people in our social world, too. Most people respond to symbolism, so even if they identify as non-spiritual, they will probably have a moving experience when presented with a small element of ceremony. For example, at my Solstice parties, I often give arriving guests a piece of paper and explain that they are welcome—but not required—to take part in a mini-ceremony later in the evening. On the paper, I ask them to write something they are grateful for, or something they want to let go of. I make it clear they won't have to share their feelings. Then a few hours later, I ring a bell to call people to the backyard. People read what they wrote or not, participate or not. The papers are burned in the grill. Everyone feels safe and has the experience they want. After we're done, there is an open moment for words and then, back to the party!

As we move through the bustle of life, we keep our eyes open for the sacred around us. Then, on days when we need clarity, when we are called to let our guard down and work with deeper issues, we return to formal ceremony. This circular motion keeps us in sync with the ever-changing path of the spiral. We may lose our balance, but by speaking our dreams to the world in the language of ceremony, resonating with beauty and enacting formal ceremony, we will always return to ourselves.

Reach into this bundle now and draw out
the two gifts I have left for you.

Here is one last shell.

It does not hold the song of a ceremony.
Instead, it is the vessel of your own unique and
gorgeous song, this song that, more than anything,
can bring you to your deeply remembered, rightful home
inside yourself, the source of your personal power.

Hold your ear close and let its energetic essence fill you.
This shell will always be with you, and someday, if not today,
you will sing your song. Maybe you will sing with your voice.
Surely you will sing with the glow of your presence,
in the truth of yourself, imperfect and yet so perfect at
the same time. The spirits of kindness will help.

The second gift is a brilliant vision of
the collective web of light.

It is what holds all of us together in
the vast ecosystem of change makers.

I cannot draw it or speak it.
I cannot describe what it sounds like,
but I can place it here, in this spot for you
to sweep into your hand and pour into your heart.

Blessed Be.

BUNDLE OF STICKS:
CRIB NOTES

Bones of Ceremony Checklist

Crafting the Ceremony

- Listening to our hearts
- Responding to our hearts with intention
- Building a spirit bridge with symbols

Enacting Ceremony

- Calling ourselves to be present
- Marking our ceremonial space
- Making invocations
- Building energy
- Enacting the sacred work/fulfilling our intention
- Coming home
- Grounding
- Thanking the spirits and community
- Opening the circle and closing

Each of these elements is vital to making up the ceremony!

Different Gifts

Private Ceremony

- Allows you to be more vulnerable and express raw emotion
- Allows you to choose an intention and craft a form specific to your personal life
- Can easily shift mid-stream

Public Ceremony

- Raises large amounts of energy together
- Can utilize the power of witnessing
- Promotes relationships and community

Public Ceremony Organizer Notes

The Flow

- Listen to community voices and be a human bulletin board.
- Be aware of other local ceremonies and possibly conflicting events.
- Include families and children whenever appropriate to the intention.
- Bring in outside talent, if needed.
- The first invocation is the flyer.
- Include others in the planning, if possible.
- Intention must be clarified before choosing symbols.
- Listen to and honor everyone's ideas.
- Symbols must resonate with intention.
- Create a cheat sheet for public speaking.
- Expect a little bit of pre-ceremony insanity.
- Ride the chaos and look for messages from spirit in the unexpected.
- Use generic spiritual language for large groups.
- Clearly state the intention and how people can participate.
- Give everyone a role (no spectators).
- Be the anchor they need.
- Ceremony is not a performance.
- Ceremony is not a time for self-promotion.
- Don't allow yourself to be put on a pedestal.
- Ask for help in tending the container.
- Enjoy yourself. Don't work too hard.
- Don't forget to ground.
- Sharing food after the ceremony strengthens community.

The Mother Bone Poem

The White Bone of Sacred Space;
the Compass Bone to claim our place.

The Bone of Intention marks the way,
to reach our aim, we cannot stray.

The Bridging Bone of symbols made;
its power sings where steps are laid.

The Calling Bone will bring them here,
whose blessed kindness holds us dear.

The Bone of Passion stokes the fire,
living breath of deep desire.

The Bone of Home to kiss the ground,
embrace this life to which we're bound.

The Bone of Honor knows our name,
as we know others, just the same.

The Hollow Bone for you and me
to blend our songs in harmony.

The Mother Bone who feeds us all;
the Mother Bone who holds us.
The Mother Bone who twines the road,
and with her song unfolds us.

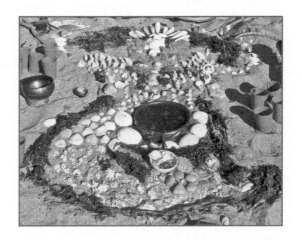

GRATITUDE

Thank you to the spirit of the owl for hanging around my room while I wrote, and for fluttering through my pages with her wings. Thank you from the bottom of my heart to Karin the book midwife, the polisher of jewels, the one who so gently and yet so firmly coaxes me to keep on, to pull down the spirits' messages from the other side and to turn them into a form that contains much shorter sentences than the ones I used to write. Thanks so much for the early reviews during my writing process—when I didn't realize I still had a long way to go—to Carol, Ian, Sherry and Steve. Thanks to all my spiritual teachers, of this world and that. Thank you to all who participated in and facilitated the Littlelight and Turtle Spirit Jam ceremonies. And thanks to my Mom, my best friend, who knows me the best and lets me be myself no matter what.

About the Author

Tasara Jen Stone has been leading public ceremonies and teaching pagan and core shamanic spirit practices in Seattle since the mid-'90s. She trained extensively in core shamanism with the Foundation for Shamanic Studies, as well as with Betsy Bergstrom, Sandra Ingerman, Leslie Conton, Tom Cowan and Bhola Banstola. She is currently living in the Seattle area, playing her flutes, writing and receiving healing clients.

Tasara has written for many publications, including: *All Things Healing, Druid's Egg, Pan Gaia, Open Ways* and the *Women of Wisdom Enews*; she had a one-year column in *Sibyl Magazine* called "There is Healing in the Garden." You can read more about her and her offerings at http://littlelight.info. Her blog, Ravenspeak, is at http://ravenspeaks.littlelight.info/.